Crochet Pillows
with Tunisian and Traditional Techniques

0 11557 00646 9

Crochet Pillows

with Tunisian and Traditional Techniques

Sharon Hernes Silverman

Photographs by Alan Wycheck

STACKPOLE
BOOKS

Published by
STACKPOLE BOOKS
5067 Ritter Road
Mechanicsburg, PA 17055
www.stackpolebooks.com

Printed in the United States of America

10 9 8 7 6 5 4 3 2

First edition

All designs © Sharon Hernes Silverman, www.SharonSilverman.com
Cover design by Caroline Stover
Standard yarn weight system chart and skill level symbols used courtesy of the Craft Yarn Council of America (CYCA), www.yarnstandards.com.
Photographs by Alan Wycheck

Library of Congress Cataloging-in-Publication Data

Silverman, Sharon Hernes.
    Crochet pillows with Tunisian and traditional techniques / Sharon Hernes Silverman ; photographs by Alan Wycheck. — 1st ed.
       p. cm.
    Includes index.
    ISBN 978-0-8117-0646-9
      1. Crocheting—Patterns. 2. Crocheting—Technique. 3. Crocheting—Tunisia. 4. Pillows. 5. Cushions. I. Title.
TT820.S5264   2011
746.43'4—dc22

                         2010026214

Contents

Acknowledgments

Many thanks to everyone who helped this book take shape.

I am grateful to those who provided supplies: Eugenia Larriera of Abuelita Yarns; Barbara Lundy Stone and Demian Savits of Blue Heron Yarns; Stacy Charles of Tahki Stacy Charles, Inc.; Emily McKeon of Denise Interchangeable Knitting and Crochet; Lijuan ("Jojo") Jing of Jojoland; Gail Callahan of Kangaroo Dyer; Amy Ross of Lion Brand Yarn Company; Dave Van Stralen of Louet North America; JoAnne Turcotte of Plymouth Yarn Company, Inc.; and Juliana Mulcahy and Wendy Zhang from Westing Bridge LLC for ChiaoGoo hooks.

Location photos were shot in the design studio of Mary V. Knackstedt, FASID, FIIDA—much gratitude to Mary for generously opening her beautiful interiors to us.

Thanks as always to photographer Alan Wycheck for his unparalleled visual contributions to this, our fourth book together.

I am grateful to Mark Allison, editor, and Judith M. Schnell, publisher and vice president, of Stackpole Books. Other members of the Stackpole team, Kathryn Fulton, Tracy Patterson, Beth Oberholtzer, Caroline Stover, and Jody Faulkner, also brought their editorial, design, marketing, and publishing expertise to this project.

Thanks to the Craft Yarn Council of America for permission to reprint charts, the Crochet Guild of America (CGOA) for industry information and news, and the National NeedleArts Association (TNNA) for its support of yarn industry professionals.

Anita Closic, owner of A Garden of Yarn, in Chadds Ford, Pennsylvania, has my appreciation for her ongoing encouragement and well-stocked, welcoming shop.

My interaction with other designers and crafters—in person and electronically—has been extremely valuable. Special thanks to the Ravelry correspondents who have been my cheerleaders, sounding boards, information sources, and all-around helpful colleagues.

I could not have completed this project without the support of my friends and family. Thanks to all of you for being so wonderful! This goes double for my husband, Alan, and our sons, Jason and Steven, who not only provided encouragement but also lived in a sea of crocheted pillows for many months.

How to Use This Book

This book is designed for people who are comfortable with basic crochet stitches (chain, single crochet, double crochet). Before you start the projects, please review the basic techniques in the back of the book.

If you have not done Tunisian crochet before, now is the time! I hope you will give these projects a try. Anyone with basic crocheting skills can pick up Tunisian in a jiffy. Basic Tunisian techniques are explained in the back of the book as well.

I also encourage everyone to read the section on stuffing and closing pillows. Follow the recommendations to get the best results.

The main part of the book has twenty patterns: ten that use traditional crochet techniques and ten patterns that use mainly Tunisian crochet techniques. In each section, the patterns are arranged in order of increasing difficulty. Step-by-step photos are included throughout this book to supplement the detailed instructions.

Reference material, including supplier information for yarn and hooks, appears at the end of the book. There is also a visual index in which you can see all of the projects at a glance.

Projects in Traditional Crochet

Springtime Miters

Mitered squares are like magic. They look complicated but are actually quite simple to make. Using a variegated yarn with long color runs, like this one in a pastel palette from Jojoland, allows the color changes to develop gradually, much like the hues of a spring sunrise. The contrasting solid color balances the lighter colors and emphasizes the shape—one big square on one side, four smaller ones on the other.

MEASUREMENTS

Finished size: 17 inches (43.2 centimeters) square

MATERIALS

Jojoland Rhythm, 100% wool, 1.76 ounces/50 grams, 110 yards/100 meters

Color A: M05 (pink, blue, green, purple), 3 skeins

Jojoland Baritone, 100% wool, 1.76 ounces/50 grams, 110 yards/100 meters

Color B: 269 (logan berry), 2 skeins

Crochet hook size H, 5.0 mm or size needed to obtain gauge

Stitch markers

Tapestry needle

Sewing thread to match darker yarn

Sewing needle

Pillow form, 17 inches (43.2 centimeters) square

STITCHES AND ABBREVIATIONS

Chain stitch (ch)

Fasten off (fo)

Loop (lp), loops (lps)

Right side (RS)

Single crochet (sc)

Skip (sk)

Slip stitch (sl st)

Stitch (st), stitches (sts)

Wrong side (WS)

Yarn over (yo)

GAUGE

17 stitches and 17 rows in sc/4 inches (10.2 centimeters)

For gauge swatch, ch 26.

Row 1: Sc in second ch from hook and in each ch across (26 sc). Turn.

Row 2: Ch 1. Sc in each sc across (26 sc). Turn.

Repeat Row 2 until swatch measures at least 4.5 inches (11.4 centimeters).

Pillow Front (Make 4)

With A, ch 2. Work 3 sc into second ch from hook. Mark as RS.

Row 1: Ch 1, turn. Sc in first st, 3 sc in next sc, sc in last st.

> **NOTE** Each row is worked with a sc in each st up to the middle, 3 sc in the middle st, then 1 sc in each remaining st. The photo shows the center st marked.

Continue through row 14 (29 st). When 2 lps remain in last sc, switch to B. Do not fasten off A.

Work 2 rows B in pattern, switching to A in last st of second row.

Continue 2 rows A, 2 rows B. When there are three stripes of B (49 sts), continue with A only. Cut B. Continue with A, finishing with a WS row that has 77 stitches. Fo.

For each square, use tapestry needle to weave in ends. Lightly steam block the square. With RS facing, join B in one corner. Ch 1. Sc all the way around, working 2-3 sc in corners so they are flat and square. Join to first st with sl st. Fo. Weave in ends. Block again if necessary.

Pillow Back

Work as for the front with the following changes: Use only A through Row 24 (49 sts). The dark stripes will begin here, corresponding to where the stripes ended on the front squares. Once you start the dark stripes, do 2 rows B, 4 rows A, and repeat, ending with A on row that has 157 stitches. Fo.

With tapestry needle, weave in ends. Lightly steam block.

With RS facing you, join B in corner. Ch 1. Sc evenly around, working 2-3 sc in corners so they are flat and square. Join to first st with sl st. Fo. Weave in ends. Block again if necessary.

Assembly

Arrange the four small squares in a pattern you like. The photo shows one idea; you could also line up the dark stripes or put them all toward the outside corners.

Using matching thread and sewing needle, sew squares together with RS up and the squares lying next to each other. Pick up one loop from each side. Knot thread; weave excess through to wrong side.

Lay the pillow top and bottom together, RS outward. Join B in one corner. Ch 1. Sc around 3 sides. Insert pillow form. Sc around remaining side. Join to first st with sl st. Fo. Weave in ends.

Sophisticated Chevrons

SKILL LEVEL

EASY

Classic neutrals—black, white, pewter, linen—in fine-gauge yarn elevate this simple chevron pattern to a high level of elegance. Use this pillow with others in similar colors for an eye-catching grouping.

The pillow is made in one piece, starting and ending on the back.

MEASUREMENTS

Finished size: 14 inches (35.6 centimeters) wide by 11 inches (27.9 centimeters) high

MATERIALS

Louet Gems #2 fine/sport weight, 100% merino wool, 3.5 ounces/100 grams, 225 yards/205 meters

Color A: Black (80-2223-29/9), 1 skein

Color B: Pewter (80-2433-18/10), 2 skeins

Color C: Linen Gray (80-2363-19/02), 1 skein

Color D: White (80-2703-18/8), 1 skein

Crochet hook size F, 3.75 mm or size needed to obtain gauge

Tapestry needle

Pillow form 11 inches (27.9 centimeters) by 14 inches (35.6 centimeters)

STITCHES AND ABBREVIATIONS

Chain stitch (ch)

Fasten off (fo)

Loop (lp), loops (lps)

Right side (RS)

Single crochet (sc)

Skip (sk)

Stitch (st), stitches (sts)

Yo (yarn over)

GAUGE (BLOCKED)

Three complete chevrons (apex to apex) and 22 rows/4.5 inches (11.4 centimeters). For gauge swatch, ch 46. Work in pattern until swatch measures 5 inches (12.7 centimeters) blocked. It is important to block your swatch to obtain a correct measurement.

Pillow

With A, ch 112.

> **NOTE** The chevron stitch is made by working 3 sc in one st at the apex of the chevron and skipping 2 sts to create a trough at the base. The diagram below shows the placement of the stitches.

Row 1: Work 2 sc into second ch from hook. *Sc into each of next 4 ch, sk 2 ch, sc into each of the next 4 ch, 3 sc into next ch. Repeat from * ending with only 2 sc into last ch. Turn.

Row 2: Ch 1. Work 2 sc into first st. *Sc into each of next 4 sts, sk 2 sts, sc into each of next 4 sts, 3 sc into next st. Repeat from * ending last repeat with 2 sc into last st. Do not work into turning ch. Turn.

Rows 3–8: Repeat Row 2, changing to B when 2 lps remain at end of Row 8.

Rows 9–36: Work 6 rows in B, 2 rows in C, 4 rows in D, 2 rows in C, 6 rows in B, 8 rows in A.

Repeat Rows 9–36 twice more.

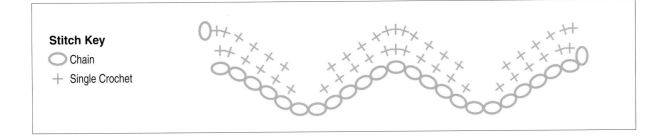

Stitch Key
◯ Chain
+ Single Crochet

Concluding rows: Work 6 rows in B, 2 rows in C, 4 rows in D, 2 rows in C, 6 rows in B. Fo.

Finishing and Assembly

With tapestry needle, weave in ends. Lightly steam block.

To prepare pillow for assembly, fold with the RS inside. The first and last rows should be touching, with the chevrons nestling together. The color stripes on the front and back should line up. The place where the first and last rows meet may not be across the exact center of the pillow (as measured from top to bottom); that's okay. With tapestry needle and yarn C, sew side seams together. Weave in ends.

Turn pillow RS out. Insert pillow form. With tapestry needle and yarn B, sew beginning and last row together to close pillow.

Woven Floor Pillow

SKILL LEVEL

EASY

This pillow is perfect for lounging. It works up quickly with chunky yarn and a large hook.

Customize your pillow by choosing your own arrangement of colors for the woven stripes. Stick with one color for a subtle look, or use multiple colors in each channel to add punch.

MEASUREMENTS

Finished size: 17.5 inches (44.5 centimeters) wide by 21.5 inches (54.6 centimeters) high.

MATERIALS

Plymouth Yarn Encore Chunky, 75% acrylic 25% wool, 3.5 ounces/100 grams, 143 yards/130.7 meters

Color A: 204 (dark green), 4 skeins

Color B: 1385 (hot pink), 1 skein

Color C: 1382 (yellow), 1 skein

Color D: 1386 (red), 1 skein

Color E: 133 (blue), 1 skein

Crochet hook size I, 5.5 mm or size needed to obtain gauge

Tapestry needle

Pillow form or dense foam, 17.5 inches (44.5 centimeters) wide by 21.5 inches (54.6 centimeters) high. If you use dense foam, it should be approximately 2 inches (5.1 centimeters) thick.

STITCHES AND ABBREVIATIONS

Chain stitch (ch)

Fasten off (fo)

Half double crochet (hdc)

Loop (lp), loops (lps)

Right side (RS)

Single crochet (sc)

Skip (sk)

Slip stitch (sl st)

Stitch (st), stitches (sts)

Wrong side (WS)

Yarn over (yo)

GAUGE

10 stitches and 10 rows in hdc/4 inches (10.2 centimeters)

For gauge swatch, ch 16. Hdc in third ch from hook and in each remaining ch. Turn.

Row 1: Ch 2 (counts as hdc). Sk base of ch. Hdc in each st across. Turn.

Repeat Row 1 until swatch is at least 4.5 inches (11.4 centimeters).

Pillow Top (Make 2)

With A, ch 60.

Row 1 (RS). Sc in second ch from hook and in each ch across. Total 59 sc. Turn.

Row 2 (WS). Ch 1. Sc in each st across.

Row 3. Ch 3 (counts as 1 hdc and 1 ch). Sk base of turning ch and next sc. *Hdc in each of next 3 st, ch 1, sk 1 st. Repeat from * across, ending with hdc in top of turning ch. Total 15 windows. Turn.

Row 4. Ch 2 (counts as 1 hdc). *Hdc in window space, hdc in each of next 3 sts. Repeat from * across, ending with hdc in top of turning ch. Total 59 hdc. Turn.

Repeat Rows 3 and 4 until pillow measures approximately 20 inches (50.8 centimeters), ending with Row 4. There should be 15 window rows from bottom to top.

Final row (RS): Ch 1. Sc in each st across. Total 59 sc. Fo.

Finishing

With tapestry needle, weave in ends. Lightly steam block.

Weaving

Cut lengths of contrasting-color yarn approximately 30 inches (76.2 centimeters). Cut the following number of lengths:

16 B

16 C

16 D

12 E

If the yarn is curly, lightly steam block it before weaving.

Weave a pair of yarn lengths through each set of windows, starting and ending with yarn coming out the top of the RS.

Use this order:

A, B, C, D, A, B, C, D, A, B, C, D, A, B, C.

Don't knot the yarn yet; just leave the ends hanging out.

Assembly

Place pillow top and bottom together with RS out, being sure to match up woven colors (unless you purposely don't want to). Join A in corner through both thicknesses. Sc around three sides, moving the fringe out of your way as you go. Insert pillow form. Sc around remaining side. Fo. Pull end through to inside of pillow.

Tie top and bottom of fringe together in a knot at each end. Trim to an even length.

Loop-de-loop

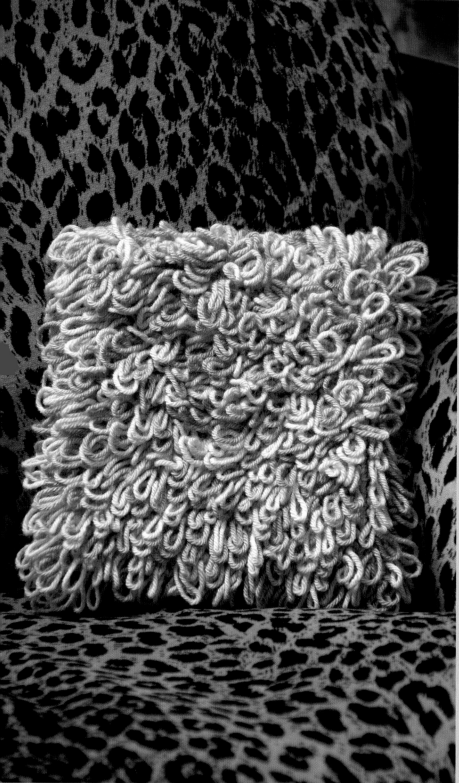

The loop stitch is a variation on single crochet, with the yarn pulled up to the desired size in the middle of the stitch. Variegated green yarn from Kangaroo Dyer adds to this loopy pillow's three-dimensional look. Pair it with the Furry Fun pillow (page 16) for an exotic set.

MEASUREMENTS

Finished size: 10 inches (25.4 centimeters) square

MATERIALS

Kangaroo Dyer, 50% merino, 50% silk, 3.5 ounces/
100 grams, 300 yards/275 meters

Color: Green variegated, 1 skein

Crochet hook size H, 5.0 mm or size needed to
obtain gauge

Tapestry needle

Pillow form 10 inches (25.4 centimeters) square

STITCHES AND ABBREVIATIONS

Chain stitch (ch)

Fasten off (fo)

Loop (lp), loops (lps)

Loop stitch (lp st)

Right side (RS)

Single crochet (sc)

Skip (sk)

Slip stitch (sl st)

Stitch (st), stitches (sts)

Wrong side (WS)

Yarn over (yo)

GAUGE

13 stitches and 20 rows in sc/4 inches
(10.2 centimeters)

For gauge swatch, ch 17.

Row 1: Sc in second ch from hook and in each ch
across (16 sc). Turn.

Row 2: Ch 1. Sc in each sc across (16 sc). Turn.

Repeat Row 2 until swatch measures at least
4.5 inches (11.4 centimeters).

Special Stitch

Loop stitch (lp st):

1. Insert hook as for sc.

2. Using a finger of your free hand, pull up the yarn to
form a lp approximately 1 inch (2.5 centimeters) tall.

3. Put hook behind both both strands of the lp near the base and pull up both strands, leaving the loopy end sticking out the back.

4. Release lp from your finger. Using working yarn (not tall lp), yo, pull through all 3 lps.

Pillow Front

Ch 31.

Row 1 (RS): Sc in second ch from hook and in each ch across. Total 30 sc. Turn.

Row 2: Ch 1. Work lp st in each sc across. Lps will appear on the opposite side (RS) of the fabric. Turn.

Row 3: Ch 1. Sc in each st across. Turn.

Repeat Rows 2 and 3 until pillow front measures 9 inches (22.9 centimeters).

Final Row: Ch 1. Sc in each st across. Work 3 sc in corner, then sc evenly around remaining sides with 3 sc in each corner. Join to first sc with sl st. Fo.

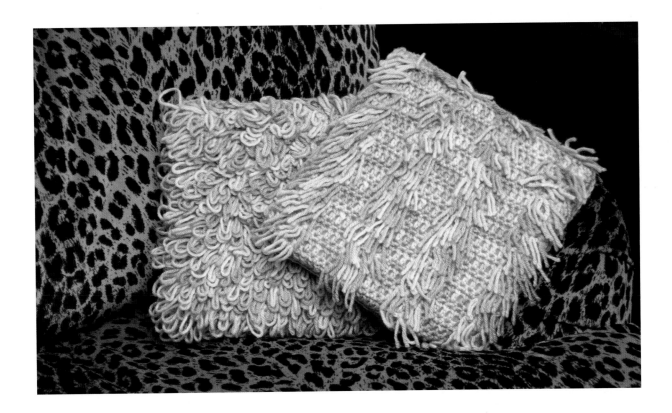

Pillow Back

Ch 31.

Row 1 (RS): Sc in second ch from hook and in each ch across. Total 30 sc. Turn.

Row 2: Ch 1. Sc in each sc across. Turn.

Repeat Row 2 until pillow back measures 9 inches (22.9 centimeters), finishing with a WS row.

Final Row: Ch 1. Sc in each st across. Work 3 sc in corner, then sc evenly around remaining sides with 3 sc in each corner. Join to first sc with sl st. Fo.

Finishing

With tapestry needle, weave in ends. Gently steam block.

Assembly

Line up pillow top and bottom so stitches are oriented the same way, with RS facing out. Attach yarn in any corner, going through both thicknesses. Sc evenly around three sides of pillow. Insert pillow form, making sure corners are full. Sc along fourth side. Join to first st with sl st. Fo. Pull end through to inside of pillow.

Furry Fun

The fur stitch is simply the loop stitch with the loops snipped. Working the fur in columns creates an interesting counterpoint between raised and flat areas. Group this with the Loop-de-loop pillow (page 12) to jazz up any room.

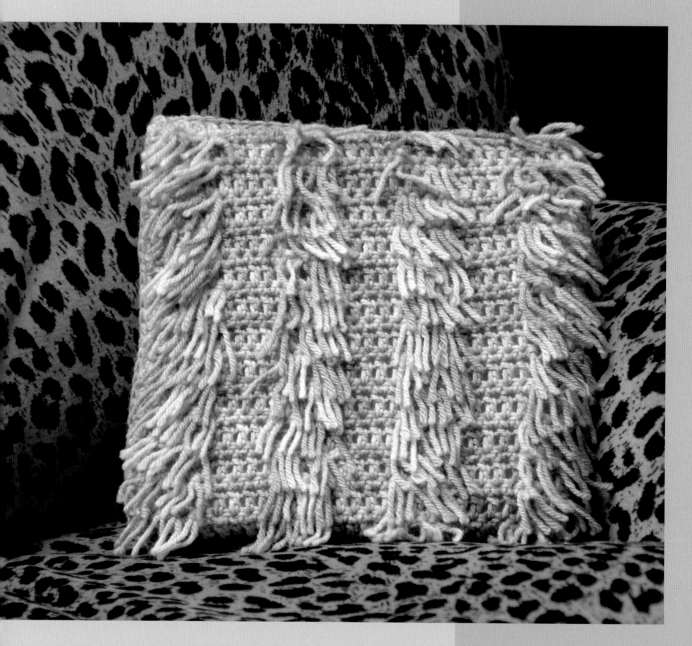

MEASUREMENTS

Finished size: 10 inches (25.4 centimeters) square

MATERIALS

Kangaroo Dyer, 50% merino, 50% silk, 3.5 ounces/
100 grams, 300 yards/275 meters

Color: Green variegated, 1 skein

Crochet hook size H, 5.0 mm or size needed to
obtain gauge

Tapestry needle

Pillow form, 10 inches (25.4 centimeters) square

STITCHES AND ABBREVIATIONS

Chain stitch (ch)

Double crochet (dc)

Fasten off (fo)

Loop (lp), loops (lps)

Loop stitch (lp st)

Right side (RS)

Single crochet (sc)

Skip (sk)

Slip stitch (sl st)

Stitch (st), stitches (sts)

Wrong side (WS)

Yarn over (yo)

GAUGE

13 stitches and 20 rows in sc/4 inches
(10.2 centimeters)

For gauge swatch, ch 17.

Row 1: Sc in second ch from hook and in each
ch across (16 sc). Turn.

Row 2: Ch 1. Sc in each sc across (16 sc). Turn.

Repeat Row 2 until swatch measures at least
4.5 inches (11.4 centimeters).

Special Stitch

Loop Stitch (lp st)

1. Insert hook as for sc.
2. Using a finger of your free hand, pull up the yarn to
   form a lp approximately 1 inch (2.5 centimeters) tall.
3. Put hook behind both strands of the lp near the base
   and pull up both strands, leaving the loopy end sticking out the back.

4. Release lp from your finger. Using working yarn (not
   lp), yo, pull through all 3 lps.

> **NOTE** This is the same sequence illustrated on
> pages 13 and 14. The loop stitches are worked on
> the WS because the loops form on the back of the
> stitch and will appear on the RS.

This pillow uses double crochet stitches on the inter-
vening rows of the pillow front, not single crochet like the
Loop-de-loop pillow. The backs of both pillows are worked
in single crochet.

Pillow Front

Ch 36.

Row 1 (RS): Sk 3 ch (counts as 1 dc), dc into next ch and
each ch to end. Turn.

Row 2: Ch 1. Sc into each of first 2 sts. *Lp st into each
of next 4 sts, sc into each of next 4 sts. Repeat from * to
last 2 sts, sc into each of last 2 sts including top of turning
ch. Turn.

Row 3: Ch 3 (counts as 1 dc). Do not work a st at the
base of the chs. Dc into next st and each st across. Turn.

Repeat Rows 2 and 3 until pillow front measures 9
inches (22.9 centimeters), finishing with Row 2.

Final Row: Ch 1. Sc in each st across. Work 3 sc in corner, then sc evenly around remaining sides with 3 sc in each
corner. Join to first sc with sl st. Fo.

Create Fur

Cut each lp at the apex to make fur.

Pillow Back

Ch 33.

Row 1 (RS): Sc in second ch from hook and in each ch across. Total 32 sc. Turn.

Row 2: Ch 1. Sc in each sc across. Turn.

Repeat Row 2 until pillow back measures 9 inches (22.9 centimeters), finishing with a WS row.

Final Row: Ch 1. Sc in each st across. Work 3 sc in corner, then sc evenly around remaining sides with 3 sc in each corner. Join to first sc with sl st. Fo.

Finishing

With tapestry needle, weave in ends. Gently steam block.

Assemble Pillow

Line up pillow top and bottom so stitches are oriented the same way, and with the RS out. Attach yarn in any corner, going through both thicknesses. Sc evenly around three sides of pillow. Insert pillow form, making sure corners are full. Sc along fourth side. Join to first st with sl st. Fo. Pull end through to inside of pillow.

Cable Columns

SKILL LEVEL

■■■▢

INTERMEDIATE

Elongated cables, four stitches wide, form stately columns in this pillow, worked in Tahki Yarns Lana. The excellent definition this yarn provides makes it ideal for relief stitches like cables. The cording around the edge is reverse single crochet.

MEASUREMENTS

Finished size: 16 inches (40.6 centimeters) square

MATERIALS

Tahki Yarns Lana, 100% merino wool, 1.75 ounces/
50 grams, 92 yards/83 meters

Color: 002 (Rosewood), 5 skeins

Crochet hook size J, 6.0 mm or size needed to
obtain gauge

Tapestry needle

Pillow form, 16 inches (40.6 centimeters) square

STITCHES AND ABBREVIATIONS

Chain stitch (ch)

Double crochet (dc)

Fasten off (fo)

Front post double crochet (fpdc)

Loop (lp), loops (lps)

Reverse single crochet (rsc)

Right side (RS)

Single crochet (sc)

Skip (sk)

Slip stitch (sl st)

Stitch (st), stitches (sts)

Wrong side (WS)

Yarn over (yo)

GAUGE

14 sc stitches and 15 rows/4 inches (10.2 centimeters)
For gauge swatch, ch 21.

Foundation row: Sc in second ch from hook and
in each ch across. Total 20 sc. Turn.

Row 1: Ch 1. Sc in each sc across. Turn.

Repeat Row 1 until swatch measures at least
4.5 inches (11.4 centimeters).

Special Stitches

Front post double crochet

1. Yo. Insert hook from right to left around the post of
the stitch two rows below.

The hook will start and end at the front of the work. Tip:
Tilt the top of the work slightly away from you to make it
easier for the hook to go behind the post and come out to
the front again.

2. Complete the dc.

Reverse single crochet

1. With hook pointing downwards, insert hook in the
next stitch to the right (for right-handers; left for left-
handers). This is the opposite direction from how sc is
usually worked. Keep the working end of the yarn
behind the fabric.

2. Yo, pull up lp, yo, pull through 2 lps (rsc made). The
twisting action of the hook twists the loops also. After a
few sts, you will see the corded pattern begin to appear.

Pillow Front

Ch 47.

Row 1 (RS): Sc in second ch from hook and in each ch across. Total 46 sc. Turn.

Row 2: Ch 1. Sc in each sc across. Total 46 sc. Turn.

Rows 3 and 4: Repeat Row 2.

Row 5 (RS, set up cable): Ch 1. Sc in each of first 3 sc. Fpdc around sc 2 rows below. Sk sc behind the fpdc. Sc in next 3 sc. *Fpdc around each of next 4 sc 2 rows below. Sc in each of next 3 sc. Repeat from * to last 4 sts. Fpdc around sc 2 rows below. Sc in last 3 sc. Turn.

Row 6 (WS): Ch 1. Sc in each st across. When working behind the cable, make sure your sc are in the top of the sts, not in the sts that were skipped on the previous row. Turn.

Row 7 (continue set-up): Ch 1. Sc in each of first 3 st. Fpdc around previous fpdc.

Sc in next 3 sc. *Fpdc around each of next 4 fpdc 2 rows below. Sc in next 3 sc. Repeat from * to last 4 sts. Fpdc around fpdc 2 rows below. Sc in last 3 sc. Turn.

Row 8: Repeat Row 6.

Row 9 (RS, create cable crossover): Ch 1. Sc in each of first 3 st. Fpdc around previous fpdc. Sc in next 3 sc.

NOTE To create the crossover in the 4-st cable, you will work fpdc in this order: 3, 4, 1, 2. St 3 is marked in the photo below.

Sk 2 fpdc. *Fpdc around each of the next 2 sts.

Now go back to the skipped sts. Fpdc around the first skipped st and then the second skipped st.

Sc in next 3 sc. Repeat from * to last 4 sts. Fpdc around fpdc below. Sc in last 3 sc. Turn.

Row 10: Repeat Row 6.

Row 11 (RS, straighten out cable): Ch 1. Turn. Sc in each of first 3 sts. Fpdc around fpdc below. Sc in each of next 3 sc. *Spread out the cable sts so you can see the 2 fpdc sts that are underneath.

> **NOTE** These stitches are worked in order, 1, 2, 3, 4. St 1 is marked in the photo below.

Fpdc around each of those 2 fpdc sts and each of the next 2 fpdc sts (the ones on top). Sc in each of next 3 sc. Repeat from * to last 4 sts. Fpdc around fpdc below.

Sc in each of last 3 sc. Turn.

Row 12: Repeat Row 6. The photo shows what the back of the fabric looks like behind the cables.

Rows 13-52: Repeat Rows 5-12 five times.

Rows 53 and 54: Repeat Rows 5 and 6.

Row 55: Ch 1. Sc in each st across.

Row 56: Ch 1. Sc in each st across.

Row 57: Ch 1. Sc in each st around the perimeter of the pillow, working working 2-3 sc in each corner so the corners are flat. Join to first st with sl st. Fo.

Pillow Back

Ch 47.

Row 1 (RS): Sc in second ch from hook and in each ch across. Total 46 sc. Turn.

Row 2: Ch 1. Sc in each sc across. Total 46 sc. Turn.

Repeat Row 2 until pillow measures 15 inches (38.1 centimeters).

Final row: Ch 1. Sc in each st around the perimeter of the pillow, working 2-3 sc in each corner so the corners are flat. Join to first st with sl st. Fo.

Finishing

Using tapestry needle, weave in ends. Lightly steam block pieces if desired.

Assembly

Row 1: Arrange top and bottom with RS out. Join yarn through both thicknesses in any corner. Ch 1. Sc all the way around three sides through both thicknesses. Insert pillow form. Close fourth side with sc through both thicknesses. Join to first st with sl st.

Row 2: Do not turn. Ch 1. Rsc around entire pillow. Join to first st with sl st. Fo. Pull end through to inside of pillow to hide it.

Sunburst

SKILL LEVEL

INTERMEDIATE

This exuberant round pillow with its bright colors and curly rays will wake up any decor. The spiral is worked with two strands held together—first the same color, then two different colors. Springy embellishments give this project even more zing.

MEASUREMENTS

Finished size: 12 inches (30.5 centimeters) in diameter plus curly rays

MATERIALS

Filati Cervinia Caprice (distributed by Plymouth Yarn Company), 100% acrylic, 1.75 ounces/50 grams, 145 yards/133 meters

Color A: Orange (1517), 1 skein

Color B: Yellow (1516), 1 skein

Color C: Purple (1641), 1 skein

Color D: Hot pink (1585), 1 skein

Color E: Darkest navy (1552), 1 skein

Crochet hook size J, 6.0 mm or size needed to obtain gauge

Stitch marker

Tapestry needle

Pillow form, 12 inches (30.5 centimeters) in diameter

STITCHES AND ABBREVIATIONS

Chain stitch (ch)

Fasten off (fo)

Increase (inc)

Loop (lp), loops (lps)

Single crochet (sc)

Slip stitch (sl st)

Stitch (st), stitches (sts)

Yo (yarn over)

GAUGE

6 rounds with 2 strands held together/4 inches (10.2 centimeters) in diameter. For gauge swatch, work in pattern until swatch is at least 4.5 inches (11.4 centimeters) in diameter.

Pillow (Make 2)

The pillow is worked in a spiral (no joins) with two strands throughout. First two strands of the same color are used, then one strand each of two colors, then two of the second color, and so on. When working two strands of the same color, you can pull yarn from the inside and the outside of the skein simultaneously (remove label first).

It is important that the pillow be neatly round. If your pillow starts to "cup," increase slightly more frequently than the pattern indicates. If your pillow starts to "ruffle," increase slightly less frequently than the pattern indicates. Whatever adjustments you make, switch to the next color when you come to the beginning of the spiral.

Foundation round: With 2 strands A held together, ch 2. Work 5 sc in second ch from hook.

NOTE Do not turn. Right side always faces you.

Round 1: Work 2 sc into each st from foundation round. Mark the top of the first st you make. Work the final st until 2 lps remain on hook; cut one strand A, finish st with 1 strand A and 1 strand B. Total 10 sc.

Round 2: Work 2 sc in each st. Repeat to end of round until 2 lps of final st remain. Cut A, finish st with 2 strands B. Total 20 sc.

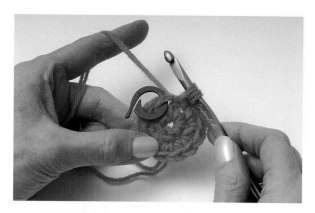

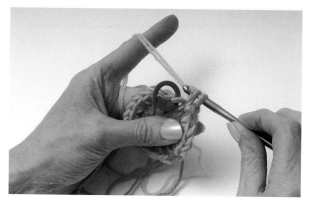

Round 3: *Work 1 sc in first st, 2 sc in next st. Repeat from * to end of round until 2 lps of final st remain. Cut one strand B, finish st with 1 strand B and 1 strand C. Total 30 sc.

Round 4: *Work 1 sc in each of first 2 sts, 2 sc in next st. Repeat from * to end of round until 2 lps of final st remain. Cut B, finish with 2 strands C. Total 40 sc.

Round 5: Work 1 sc in each st around until 2 lps of final st remain. Cut one strand C, finish with 1 strand C and one strand D. Total 40 sc.

Round 6: *Work 1 sc in each of first 3 sts, 2 sc in next st. Repeat from * around until 2 lps of final st remain. Cut C, finish with 2 strands D. Total 50 sc.

Round 7: *Work 1 sc in each of first 4 sts, 2 sc in next st. Repeat from * around until 2 lps of final st remain. Cut one strand of D, finish with 1 strand D and 1 strand E. Total 60 sc.

Round 8: Work 1 sc in each st around until 2 lps of final st remain. Cut D, finish with 2 strands E. Total 60 sc.

Round 9: *Work 1 sc in each of first 5 sts, 2 sc in next st. Repeat from * around until 2 lps of final st remain. Cut one strand of E, finish with 1 strand E and 1 strand A. Total 70 sc.

Round 10: Work 1 sc in each st around until 2 lps of final st remain. Cut E, finish with 2 strands A. Total 70 sc.

Round 11: *Work 1 sc in each of first 6 sts, 2 sc in next st. Repeat from * around until 2 lps of final st remain. Cut one strand of A, finish with 1 strand A and 1 strand B. Total 80 sc.

NOTE Continue to mark the first st of every round.

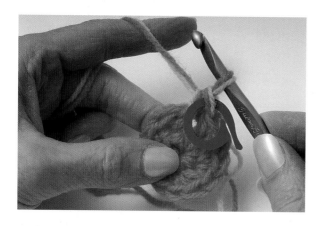

Round 12: *Work 1 sc in each of first 7 sts, 2 sc in next st. Repeat from * around until 2 lps of final st remain. Cut A, finish with 2 strands B. Total 90 sc.

Round 13: Work 1 sc in each st around until 2 lps of final st remain. Cut one strand B, finish with 1 strand B and 1 strand C. Total 90 sc.

Round 14: *Work 1 sc in each of first 8 sts, 2 sc in next st. Repeat from * around until 2 lps of final st remain. Cut B, finish with 2 strands C. Total 100 sc.

Round 15: Work 1 sc in each st around until 2 lps of final st remain. Cut one strand C, finish with 1 strand C and one strand D. Total 100 sc.

Round 16: *Work 1 sc in each of first 9 sts, 2 sc in next st. Repeat from * around until 2 lps of final st remain. Cut C, finish with 2 strands D. Total 110 sc.

Round 17: Work 1 sc in each st around until 2 lps of final st remain. Cut one strand D, finish with 1 strand D and 1 strand E. Total 110 sc.

Round 18: *Work 1 sc in each of first 10 sts, 2 sc in next st. Repeat from * around until 2 lps of final st remain. Cut D, finish with 2 strands E. Total 120 sc.

Round 19: Work 1 sc in each st around. Total 120 sc. Join to first st of round with sl st. Fo.

Finishing

With tapestry needle, weave in ends. Gently steam block fabric to flatten out the curl and make sure the piece is neat and round.

Add Sun Rays (Make 2 of Each Color)

Use 1 strand. Leaving a 4-inch tail, ch 20. Work 5 dc in second ch from hook and each ch across.

Fo, leaving a 4-inch tail.

NOTE Twist the finished rays to make them curl properly.

Arrange rays evenly around WS of one of the pillow pieces. Align them so the ends will be hidden but the rays will stick out. Pull one tail end through a few stitches, the other tail end through different but nearby stitches. Knot the tail ends together. Weave in remaining ends.

Assembly

With RS out, join double strand of E anywhere on perimeter, going through both thicknesses. Sc all the way around, moving sun rays out of the way as you go. Stop when halfway around and insert the pillow form, then continue with sc to close pillow. Fo. Pull ends through to inside.

Spiral Flower

SKILL LEVEL

INTERMEDIATE

Six spiral shell motifs are joined together to make this whimsical accent pillow with a solid color center. Display it on a chair, in a vase, or even nestled in a basket of ostrich eggs for a happy little surprise.

MEASUREMENTS

Finished size: 9 inches (22.9 centimeters) in diameter

MATERIALS

Blue Heron Silk/Merino, 50% silk 50% merino,
4 ounces/113 grams, 375 yards/343 meters

Color A: (Ocean), 1 skein

Tahki Stacy Charles Cotton Classic, 100% mercerized
cotton, 1.75 ounces/50 grams, 108 yards/100
meters

Color: 3947 (Dark Red-Violet), 1 skein

Crochet hook size H, 5.0 mm or size needed to obtain
gauge

Stitch marker

Tapestry needle

Straight pins

Sewing thread to match B

Sewing needle

Cotton batting or polyfill, approximately 3 ounces

STITCHES AND ABBREVIATIONS

Back loop only (blo)

Chain stitch (ch)

Double crochet (dc)

Fasten off (fo)

Half double crochet (hdc)

Right side (RS)

Single crochet (sc)

Skip (sk)

Slip stitch (sl st)

Treble crochet (tr)

Stitch (st), stitches (sts)

WS (wrong side)

Yarn over (yo)

GAUGE

Each motif should measure 4 inches (10.2
centimeters) across widest point.

For gauge swatch, work one motif. If it is the desired
gauge, use it as the first of the seven motifs
needed for the pillow.

Special Stitches

Working into the back loop only.

Instead of inserting your hook under both threads of a
stitch, insert it only under the thread that is farthest from
you. The unworked front loops will create a ridge.

Shell Motif (Make 7)

NOTE The motif is not turned. The RS is always
facing you.

With A, ch 4. Sl st in first ch to join into ring.

Round 1: Work 8 sc into ring. Continuing in spiral, work
[2 hdc in blo of next st] 5 times, [2 dc in blo of next st] 9
times, [2 tr in blo of next st] 7 times, [1 tr in blo of next st,
2 tr in blo of next st] 7 times, 1 tr in blo of next st, 2 tr in
blo of next st, 1 tr in blo of next st. Fo.

Top Center

The bottom center consists of one of the shell motifs you already made. For the top, use 2 strands of B held together. You will create a bowl-like shape.

Foundation round: With 2 strands B held together, ch 2. Work 5 sc in second ch from hook.

> **NOTE** The top is not turned. The RS is always facing you.

Round 1: Work 2 sc into each st from foundation round (through both lps, not blo). Mark the top of the first st you make. Total 10 sc.

> **NOTE** Continue to mark the first st of every round.

Round 2: Work 2 sc in each st. Total 20 sc.

Round 3: *Work 1 sc in first st, 2 sc in next st. Repeat from * to end of round. Total 30 sc.

Round 4: * Work 1 sc in each of first 2 sts, 2 sc in next st. Repeat from * to end of round. Total 40 sc.

Round 5: Work 1 sc in each st around. Total 40 sc.

Round 6: *Work 1 sc in each of first 3 sts, 2 sc in next st. Repeat from * around. Total 50 sc. Circle will start to "cup."

Round 7: *Work 1 sc in each of first 4 sts, 2 sc in next st. Repeat from * around. Total 60 sc.

Round 8: Work 1 sc in each st around. Total 60 sc.

Round 9: Repeat Round 8.

Round 10: Repeat Round 8. Fo.

Finishing

With tapestry needle, weave in ends. Lightly steam block the motifs. It is not necessary to block the purple circle.

Assembly

1. Arrange six motifs, RS up, as shown.

2. Pin in place.

3. With sewing thread and needle, join motifs into flower shape. Remove pins.

4. Flip joined motifs over so the WS is up. Place seventh motif over the middle of the flower, with its RS out. Sew in place.

5. Flip flower back over. Arrange purple center, RS up. Pin in place.

6. Sew three-quarters of the way around. Stuff with batting.

7. Continue sewing the center closed, adding additional batting if necessary. It should be plump.

8. Knot thread and cut. Pull end into center of pillow to hide it.

Thanksgiving Bounty

SKILL LEVEL

■■■■
EXPERIENCED

The colors and textures of Thanksgiving take center stage in this project. Baby merino lace from Uruguay-based Abuelita Yarns is as soft as can be, with rich, deeply saturated colors. Maybe the quality is so good because, as the label says, Abuelita's products come from "healthy and well-treated sheep."

Spike stitches are made by inserting the hook one or more rows below the current row, then pulling up the yarn to full height. This pillow uses a series of spikes at varying heights to create the arrowhead effect. The back is worked in single crochet, alternating solid and variegated yarn. Fringe adds a little motion to the finished project.

MEASUREMENTS

Finished size: 14 inches (35.6 centimeters) wide by 10 inches (25.4 centimeters) high, plus fringe

MATERIALS

Abuelita Baby Merino Lace, 100% merino wool, 3.5 ounces/100 grams, 420 yards/384 meters

Color A: Damasco orange (1475), 1 skein

Color B: Brown variegated (6M23), 1 skein

Crochet hook size G, 4.25 mm or size needed to obtain gauge

Tapestry needle

Pillow form 10 by 14 inches (25.4 by 35.6 centimeters)

STITCHES AND ABBREVIATIONS

Chain stitch (ch)

Fasten off (fo)

Loop (lp), loops (lps)

Single crochet (sc)

Slip stitch (sl st)

Spike single crochet (ssc)

Stitch (st), stitches (sts)

Yo (yarn over)

GAUGE

15 sts and 20 rows in sc with 2 strands held together /4 inches (10.2 centimeters).

For gauge swatch, using 2 strands held together, ch 21. Sc in second ch from hook and in each ch across. Total 20 sc. Turn.

Row 1. Ch 1. Sc in each st. Turn.

Repeat Row 1 until swatch measures at least 4.5 inches (11.4 centimeters).

NOTE The pillow is worked with two strands held together throughout. You can pull yarn from the inside and the outside of the skein simultaneously (remove label first).

Special Stitches

Spike Single Crochet (ssc). Insert hook below next st one or more rows down, as indicated in the abbreviation (ssc1, ssc2, ssc3, and so on), yo, pull lp up to height of current row, yo, pull through both lps.

This photo shows the 0 row position, where you would ordinarily work a single crochet. For the spike stitch, you will skip this position and work one row below.

Here is the entry position for a ssc1, a spike stitch that is worked one row below the usual row.

When completing the stitch, pull the yarn up so it is the same height as all of the stitches on that row. Make sure it is not bunching up the fabric.

Here is the entry position for a ssc2, a spike stitch that is worked two rows below the usual row.

The yarn is pulled up to the same height as all of the stitches on that row.

Here is what the front will look like.

And the back.

Pillow Front

Foundation row (RS): With 2 strands of A held together, ch 51. Sc into second ch from hook and in each ch across. Total 50 sc. Turn.

Row 1: Ch 1. Sc in each st across. Total 50 sc. Turn.

Rows 2-5: Repeat Row 1, changing to 2 strands B when 2 lps remain on hook at the end of Row 5. Turn.

Row 6: Ch 1. Sc in first st. *Ssc1, ssc2, ssc3, ssc4 in next 4 sts. Repeat from * across to last st. Sc in last st. Turn.

Rows 7-11: Ch 1. Sc in each st across. Total 50 sc. Change to A when 2 lps remain on hook at end of Row 11. Turn.

Row 12: Ch 1. Sc in first st. *Ssc4, ssc3, ssc2, ssc1 in next 4 sts. Repeat from * across to final st. Sc in final st. Turn.

NOTE The spike stitches here start with the longest one and get progressively shorter. This is opposite to the previous spike stitches, which start with the shortest one and get progressively longer.

Repeat Rows 1-12 three times, changing color before doing a spike row.

Repeat Rows 1-3. Fo.

Pillow Back

Foundation row (RS): With 2 strands of A held together, ch 51. Sc into second ch from hook and in each ch across. Total 50 sc. Turn.

Row 1: Ch 1. Sc in each st across. Total 50 sc. Turn.

Repeat Row 1 with the following colors:

4 rows A
5 rows B
2 rows A
10 rows B
3 rows A
3 rows B
6 rows A
5 rows B
1 row A
3 rows B
8 rows A
2 rows B
Fo.

Finishing

With tapestry needle, weave in ends. Gently steam block.

Assembly

With RS out, position pillow top and bottom together. Using 2 strands of B, join yarn in any corner. Ch 1. Sc evenly around three sides, working 2-3 sts in each corner so piece is square and flat. Insert pillow form. Sc remaining side closed. Join to first st with sl st. Fo. Pull end to inside of pillow.

Fringe

1. Using an 8-inch-long piece of cardboard, wrap a double strand of B around 12 times, ending where you started.
2. Cut across the bottom to give 12 paired strands of equal length.
3. Fold each pair in half.
4. Using a crochet hook, pull the folded end of one pair through each corner of the pillow from front to back.
5. Pull the cut ends through the loop in the folded end. Tighten to knot in place.
6. Place remaining fringe at the end of each row with B spike stitches, evenly spaced up the short sides.
7. Trim ends. Gently steam block fringe if desired.

3-D Squares

Tall relief stitches—as long as quintuple trebles—create raised frames around the stitches in this pillow. It takes a little practice to hold so many loops on the hook, but it's worth it for the effects those stitches create. Starting with a dark center and moving outward to lighter neutrals enhances the three-dimensional look. The back consists of single crochet.

MEASUREMENTS

Finished size: 17 inches (43.2 centimeters) wide by 15 inches (38.1 centimeters) high

MATERIALS

Louet Gems #2 fine/sport weight 100% merino wool, 3.5 ounces/100 grams, 225 yards/205 meters

Color A: Linen gray (80-2363-19/02), 1 skein

Color B: Pewter (80-2433-18/10), 1 skein

Color C: Black (80-2223-29/9), 3 skeins

Crochet hook size L, 6.5 mm or size needed to obtain gauge

Tapestry needle

Pillow form, 15 inches (38.1 centimeters) by 17 inches (43.2 centimeters)

STITCHES AND ABBREVIATIONS

Chain stitch (ch)

Double treble/raised front (dtr/rf)

Fasten off (fo)

Loop (lp), loops (lps)

Quintuple treble/raised front (quintr/rf)

Right side (RS)

Single crochet (sc)

Stitch (st), stitches (sts)

Wrong side (WS)

Yo (yarn over)

GAUGE

12 stitches and 11 rows in sc/4 inches (10.2 centimeters)

For gauge swatch, ch 17. Sc in second ch from hook and in each ch across. Total 16 sc. Turn.

Row 1: Ch 1. Sc in each sc across. Turn.

Repeat Row 1 until swatch measures 4.5 inches (11.4 centimeters).

Special Stitches

Double treble/raised front

This stitch is worked around the post 5 rows below the current row. In the pattern, you will be able to tell where to place the stitch because the color will match up.

1. Wrap yo 3 times for double treble.

2. Locate the target stitch 5 rows below.

You will work around the post of this stitch, keeping the hook to the front of the work.

3. Insert hook around post, yo, pull to front. [Yo, pull through 2 lps] 4 times. Dtr/rf completed.

The photo shows a pair of dtr/rf.

Quintuple treble/raised front

This stitch is worked around the post 9 rows below the current row. In the pattern, you will be able to tell where to place the stitch because the color will match up.

1. Wrap yo 6 times for quintuple treble.

2. Locate the target stitch 9 rows below.

You will work around the post of this stitch, keeping the hook to the front of the work.

NOTE Use your index finger to help the lps stay in place around the hook.

3. Insert hook around post, yo, pull to front. [Yo, pull through 2 lps] 7 times. Quintr/rf completed.

The photo shows a pair of completed quintr/rf.

Pillow Front

> **NOTE** Pillow is worked with 2 strands held together throughout. You can pull yarn from the inside and outside of the ball simultaneously (remove label first).

With 2 strands A, ch 55.

Row 1 (RS): Sc into second ch from hook and in each ch to end. Turn.

Row 2: Ch 1. Sc into each sc across. Change to B when 2 lps remain on hook in last st. Turn.

Rows 3–4: Repeat Row 2, changing to C when 2 lps remain at end of Row 4.

Rows 5–8: Repeat Row 2, changing to B when 2 lps remain at end of Row 8.

Row 9: With B, ch 1. Sc into each of first 3 sts, *[dtr/rf around st 5 rows below (also color B)] twice, sc into each of next 4 sts, [dtr around st 5 rows below] twice, sc into each of next 2 sts. Repeat from * across, ending with sc into last st. Turn.

Row 10: Ch 1. Sc into each st across, changing to A when 2 lps remain at end of row. Turn.

Row 11: With A, ch 1. Sc into first st, *[quintr/rf around st 9 rows below (also color A)] twice, sc into each of next 8 sts. Repeat from * to last 3 sts. [Quintr/rf around st 9 rows below] twice, sc in last st. Turn.

Row 12: Ch 1. Sc into each st across. Turn.

Repeat Rows 1-12 three times. Do not fo.

Border

Row 1: With A, ch 1. Sc around edge, working 2-3 sc in each corner so piece is square and flat. Join to first st with sl st.

Row 2: Change to B. Turn. Repeat Row 1.

Row 3: Change to C. Turn. Repeat Row 1. Fo.

Pillow Back

With two strands C, ch 55.

Row 1 (RS): Sc in second ch from hook and in each ch across. Turn.

Row 2: Ch 1. Sc in each st across. Turn.

Repeat Row 2 until back measures 14 inches (35.6 centimeters), ending with WS row. Do not fo.

Border

Ch 1. Sc around edge, working 2-3 sc in each corner so piece is square and flat. Join to first st with sl st. Fo.

Finishing

With tapestry needle, weave in ends. Gently steam block.

Assembly

Arrange pillow top and bottom, RS out. Using 2 strands C held together, join yarn in any corner. Sc through both thicknesses around three sides of pillow. Insert pillow form. Sc along fourth side. Join to first st with sl st. Fo. Pull end through to inside of pillow.

Projects in
Tunisian Crochet

Red Hot Heart

"Felting" turns wool into matted fabric by wetting, softening, and agitating the fibers so the outer scales, or cuticles, grab onto each other. The technique—accomplished quite easily in the washing machine—works beautifully to create a smooth surface for this pillow with its three-dimensional heart embellishment. You must use wool or a blend with a substantial wool content for felting to occur. Do not use acrylic or "non-shrinking" wool.

I experimented with different stitch swatches to see which one would create the smoothest fabric for the pillow surface. Tunisian simple stitch won hands down. The spiral applique is worked in regular crochet then felted before it is sewn on.

MEASUREMENTS

Finished size before felting: 18 inches (45.7 centimeters) square

Finished size after felting but before seaming: 12 inches (30.5 centimeters) square

MATERIALS

Lion Wool (article 820), 100% wool, 3 ounces/ 85 grams, 158 yards/144 meters

Color: Scarlet (#113), 2 skeins

Tunisian hook size K, 6.5 mm or size needed to obtain gauge

Crochet hook size J, 6.0 mm or one size smaller than Tunisian hook

Crochet hook size H, 5.0 mm

Tapestry needle

Straight pins

Sewing needle

Sewing thread in matching color

Pillow form 14 inches (35.6 centimeters) square

NOTE Because the size of felted pieces can vary depending on the washing machine, purchase your pillow form after felting is complete and you have measured the exact size of your felted pillow pieces. The form should be 1 to 2 inches larger than the dimensions of the felted cover so the corners will be filled completely and the pillow will be plump.

STITCHES AND ABBREVIATIONS

Chain stitch (ch)

Double crochet (dc)

Fasten off (fo)

Loop (lp), loops (lps)

Right side (RS)

Single crochet (sc)

Slip stitch (sl st)

Stitch (st), stitches (sts)

Tunisian simple stitch (Tss)

Yo (yarn over)

GAUGE (BLOCKED BUT UNFELTED)

15 stitches and 11 rows in Tunisian simple stitch/4 inches (10 centimeters). Gauge is somewhat flexible for this project.

For gauge swatch, ch 20. Work Tss for 15 rows. This stitch tends to curl for the first few rows; steam block your swatch to relax the curl before you check your gauge.

Pillow (Make 2)

With Tunisian hook, ch 64.

Foundation row forward: Insert hook in second ch from hook. Yo, pull up lp. *Insert hook in next ch, yo, pull up a lp. Repeat from * across, adding 1 lp onto hook with each st. Total 64 lps on hook.

Foundation row return: Do not turn. Yo, pull through 1 lp. *Yo, pull through 2 lps. Repeat from * until 1 lp remains on hook.

NOTE All return passes are worked this way.

Row 1: Sk first vertical bar. *Tss in next vertical bar. Repeat from * across, working last Tss into final vertical bar and the horizontal bar behind it for stability. Return.

Repeat Row 1 until pillow measures 18 inches (45.7 centimeters). Do not fo.

Stabilize Perimeter

Do not turn. Using regular crochet hook one size smaller than the Tunisian hook you used for the pillow, insert hook in second vertical bar as for Tss. Yo, pull up lp, yo, pull through 2 lps (sc made). Continue in this fashion across the row, then work 2 or 3 sc in the corner so it is square and flat. Continue working sc evenly around other three sides, again working 2 or 3 sc in each corner. When you get back to the beginning, join to first sc with sl st. Fo.

Finishing

With tapestry needle, weave in ends. Gently steam block fabric to flatten out the curl and make sure the piece is square. Unfelted pillow should measure approximately 18 inches (45.7 centimeters) square.

Spiral Rope for Heart Embellishment

With size H crochet hook, ch 104. Work 3 dc in fourth ch from hook.

Work 4 dc in next ch and in each ch to end.

Twist the rope as you go along to keep the spiral lined up.

Fo. With tapestry needle, weave in ends.

Felting

1. Set washing machine to hot wash and cold rinse.
2. You may include the pillow pieces and spiral rope in a full load of wash so you do not waste water. Do not put the items in a lingerie bag, as this can cause them to fold over and felt unevenly. Felt them all in the same load to ensure consistent shrinkage.
3. Remove pieces from washer when cycle is finished. They will look wet and a little bedraggled and may have a wet wool smell. These characteristics will disappear as the pieces dry.
4. Measure the pillow pieces. If they have not shrunk to 12 inches (30.5 centimeters) per side, wash again. You do not have to wait for the pieces to dry first, although you can refelt at that point if desired. My pillow required two trips through the washer; yours may need a different number. Do not rewash the spiral rope.
5. Place items on a clean, lintless towel. Make sure the pillow sides are straight and the corners are square. Re-twist the spiral rope if necessary so it turns evenly.
6. Let the pieces air-dry completely. Do not put them in the clothes dryer. Do not use a hair dryer. Turn the pieces occasionally to help them dry.

Assembly

1. Examine each piece to see which side looks smoother. Use that for the RS of the finished pillow.
2. Arrange the spiral rope into a heart shape on top of one RS. Pin in place.
3. Using sewing thread that matches the pillow color, sew the heart in place. Keep the stitches hidden by placing them in the part of the spiral that touches the pillow, not the part that sticks up. Remove pins.
4. Put the pillow top and bottom together, RS facing each other. Pin three sides.
5. With sewing needle and thread, whipstitch a seam along those three sides. Remove pins. Invert the pillow so it is right-side out.
6. Place pillow form inside pillow. Make sure corners of the pillow are full. Pin final side closed.
7. Sew fourth side closed. Remove pins. Knot the thread, then run the end through the inside of the pillow so it is hidden. Cut excess if necessary.

Checkerboard

Tunisian post stitches create a checkerboard pattern on this pillow. The sample is worked in two different color pairs—brown and ivory on one side, black and khaki on the other. One color from each side is used in the border to make an attractive transition from front to back.

SKILL LEVEL

EASY

MEASUREMENTS

Finished size: 18 inches (45.7 centimeters) square

MATERIALS

Plymouth Yarn Royal Llama Silk, 60% fine llama, 40% silk, 1.75 ounces/50 grams, 102 yards/ 93.3 meters

Color A: Brown (1001), 2 skeins

Color B: Ivory (1000), 2 skeins

Color C: Black (1572), 2 skeins

Color D: Khaki (1829), 2 skeins

Tunisian hook size K, 6.5 mm or size needed to obtain gauge

Crochet hook size K, 6.5 mm or size that corresponds to Tunisian hook

Tapestry needle

Pillow form, 18 inches (45.7 centimeters) square

STITCHES AND ABBREVIATIONS

Chain stitch (ch)

Fasten off (fo)

Loop (lp), loops (lps)

Right side (RS)

Single crochet (sc)

Skip (sk)

Slip stitch (sl st)

Stitch (st), stitches (sts)

Tunisian front post double crochet (Tfpdc)

Tunisian simple stitch (Tss)

Yarn over (yo)

GAUGE

12 stitches and 13 rows in pattern/4 inches (10.2 centimeters)

For gauge swatch, ch 18 and work in pattern.

Special Stitches

Tunisian front post double crochet

As with other Tunisian stitches, the Tunisian front post double crochet will add 1 lp onto the hook.

1. Locate target st. In the photo, it is the light-colored post st next to my left thumb.

2. Yo as for dc, insert hook into work.

3. Yo, pull up lp.

4. Yo, pull through 2 lps. You should have 1 more lp on the hook than when you started.

> **NOTE** Avoid the temptation to "yo, pull through 2" an additional time like you would for a dc in regular crocheting. The Tunisian fpdc omits that final step in order to add a lp onto the hook.

Pillow Side 1

With Tunisian hook and A, ch 54.

Foundation row forward: Insert hook in second ch from hook. Yo, pull up lp. 2 lps on hook. *Insert hook in next ch. Yo, pull up lp. Each st adds another lp to the hook. Repeat from * across. Total 54 lps on hook.

Return: Do not turn. Yo, pull through 1 lp. *Yo, pull through 2 lps. Repeat from * until 1 lp remains on hook.

> **NOTE** All return passes are worked this way.

Row 1: Sk first vertical bar. Tss in each st across to final st. Insert hook into vertical bar and the horizontal thread behind it for stability.

> **NOTE** Work the final st on every row this way.

Return, changing to B when there are 2 lps left on hook. Do not cut A, just let it float up the side until you need it again.

Row 2: Sk first vertical bar. Tfpdc around both strands of the vertical bar 2 rows below, *Tss in each of next 2 vertical bars 1 row below, Tfpdc around both strands of the vertical bar 2 rows below). Repeat from * across to last vertical bar, Tss in last vertical bar. Return.

Row 3: Sk first vertical bar. Tss in each st across. Return, changing to A when 2 lps remain on hook. Do not cut B, let it float up the side until you need it again.

Row 4: Sk first vertical bar. Tfpdc around both strands of the vertical bar 2 rows below, *Tss in each of next 2 vertical bars 1 row below, Tfpdc around both strands of the vertical bar 2 rows below, repeat from * across to last vertical bar, Tss in last vertical bar. Return.

Repeat Rows 1-4 until pillow measures 16 inches (40.6 centimeters).

Repeat Rows 1 and 2. Do not switch to B.

Final row (switch to regular crochet hook if desired): With A, sk first vertical bar, *insert hook in next vertical bar, yo, pull up lp, yo, pull through 2 lps (sc made). Repeat from * across to end. Work 2 or 3 sc in corner so it lays flat. Sc evenly around remaining 3 sides of pillow, working 2 or 3 sc in each corner. Join to first st with sl st. Fo.

Pillow Side 2

Make pillow as for side 1, using colors C and D.

Finishing

Using tapestry needle, weave in ends. Gently steam block if desired, being careful not to flatten the raised sts.

Assembly

With RS out, arrange pillow front and back so the ridges are oriented the same way. Use 1 strand A together with 1 strand C. Join yarn in any corner (use regular crochet hook if desired). Ch 1. Sc through both thicknesses around 3 sides of pillow. Insert pillow form.

Continue working sc down remaining side to close pillow. Join to first st with sl st. Fo. Pull ends through to inside of pillow.

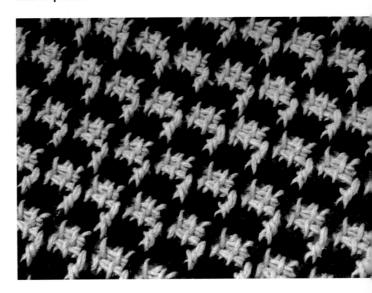

Lovejoy

The linear structure of Tunisian simple stitch provides the perfect background for cross-stitch embellishment. Dusty rose and eggplant complement each other yet contrast enough to make the embroidered messages stand out.

MEASUREMENTS

Finished size 12 inches (30.5 centimeters) wide by 10.5 inches (26.7 centimeters) high

MATERIALS

Louet Gems 100% Merino Wool light/worsted weight, 3.5 ounces/100 grams, 175 yards/160 meters

Color A: Dusty Rose (80-2644-1/9), 1 skein

Color B: Eggplant (80-2424-23/5), 1 skein

Tunisian crochet hook size H, 5.0 mm or size needed to obtain gauge

Crochet hook size H, 5.0 mm or size that corresponds to Tunisian hook

Tapestry needle

Stitch marker or safety pin

Pillow form 12 by 10.5 inches (30.5 by 26.7 centimeters)

STITCHES AND ABBREVIATIONS

Chain stitch (ch)

Fasten off (fo)

Loop (lp), loops (lps)

Single crochet (sc)

Slip stitch (sl st)

Stitch (st), stitches (sts)

Tunisian simple stitch (Tss)

Yo (yarn over)

GAUGE (BLOCKED)

17 stitches and 14 rows in Tss/ 4 inches (10 centimeters)

For gauge swatch, ch 25. Work in Tss until swatch measures at least 4.5 inches (11.4 centimeters). Block swatch before measuring gauge.

Special Stitches

Cross-stitch embellishment

Each cross-stitch consists of two parts. The underneath part of the stitch should always go from lower left to upper right; it doesn't matter which corner you start with, but that's the way the stitch should be oriented. The top part of the stitch goes from upper left to lower right across that thread. Here again, it doesn't matter in which corner you start, as long as this thread is on top and oriented properly.

To begin stitching, thread a tapestry needle with about 30 inches of yarn in contrasting color to center panel. Locate the center of the chart from right to left and the corresponding stitch on your crocheted fabric. Count up in this center position two rows above the contrasting color stripe in the center panel. Mark this stitch with a safety pin or stitch marker (the sample photo shows only the center panel, without the stripes above and below).

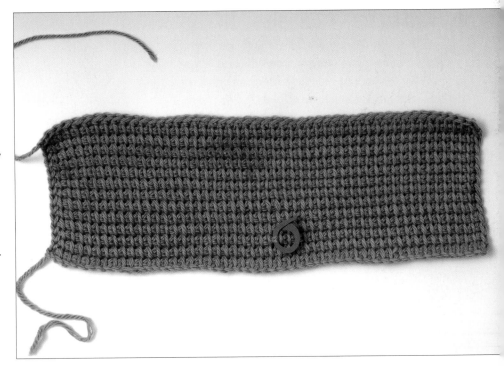

Using the chart as your guide, work the cross-stitching as shown, starting with the center stitch. This stitch will be your reference for the rest of the lettering. Remove the marker and pull up the yarn from back to front, starting at the bottom left of that square.

Be careful not to pull the stitches too tight. The fabric should stay flat.

Cross over the vertical bar to the right and the horizontal bars that represent one row. Insert the needle from front to back in that spot—it is the corresponding corner to the one where you brought up the yarn.

To start the next stitch, drop back down to the row below but stay in the same column. Bring the yarn up from back to front.

Like before, cross over the vertical bar the the right and the horizontal bars that represent one row. Insert the needle from front to back in that spot.

You can work individual cross-stitches or do them in rows. If working in rows, do all of the underneath threads first, then come back and do the top threads.

Cross over the thread and go back down in the same place you went down for the earlier stitch.

Continue in this fashion, using the chart as your guide for where to place the cross-stitches.

At the end of the yarn, weave the end in on the WS.

Pillow Front

With A, ch 51.

Foundation row forward: Insert hook in second ch from hook. Yo, pull up lp. *Insert hook in next ch, yo, pull up lp. Each st adds another lp to the hook. Repeat from * across. Total 51 lps on hook.

Return: Do not turn. Yo, pull through 1 lp. *Yo, pull through 2 lps. Repeat from * until 1 lp remains on hook.

> **NOTE** All return passes are worked this way.

Row 1: Sk first vertical bar. *Insert hook in next vertical bar, yo, pull up lp. Repeat from * across to final vertical bar. Tss in final st, inserting hook into the vertical bar and the horizontal bar behind it for stability. Return.

Rows 2-8: Repeat Row 1.

Row 9: Repeat Row 1, switching to B when 2 lps remain on hook at end of return pass.

Row 10: Repeat Row 1.

Row 11: Repeat Row 1, switching to A when 2 lps remain on hook at end of return pass.

Work 14 rows in A, 2 rows in B, 9 rows in A.

Final row (switch to regular crochet hook if desired): Sk first vertical bar. Insert hook in next vertical bar, yo, pull up lp, yo, pull through 2 lps (sc made). Continue across, working a sc in each st but inserting hook like for Tss. Fo.

Pillow Back

Make back the same way as front, reversing the positions of colors A and B.

Finishing

With tapestry needle, weave in ends. Gently steam block if desired.

Cross-Stitch Embellishment

Follow the instructions at the beginning of this project. Use charts on pages 55 and 56 as a guide for stitching the letters.

Assembly

With RS out and words oriented in the same direction, place top and bottom together. Join B through both thicknesses in any corner (use regular crochet hook if desired). Ch 1. Sc evenly around three sides of pillow. Insert pillow form. Close remaining side with sc. Join to first st with sl st. Fo. Pull end to inside of pillow.

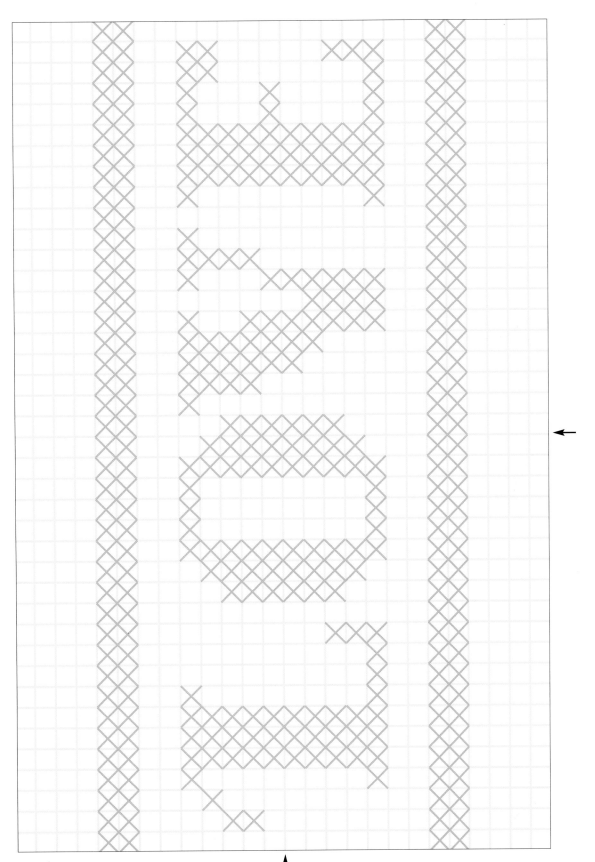

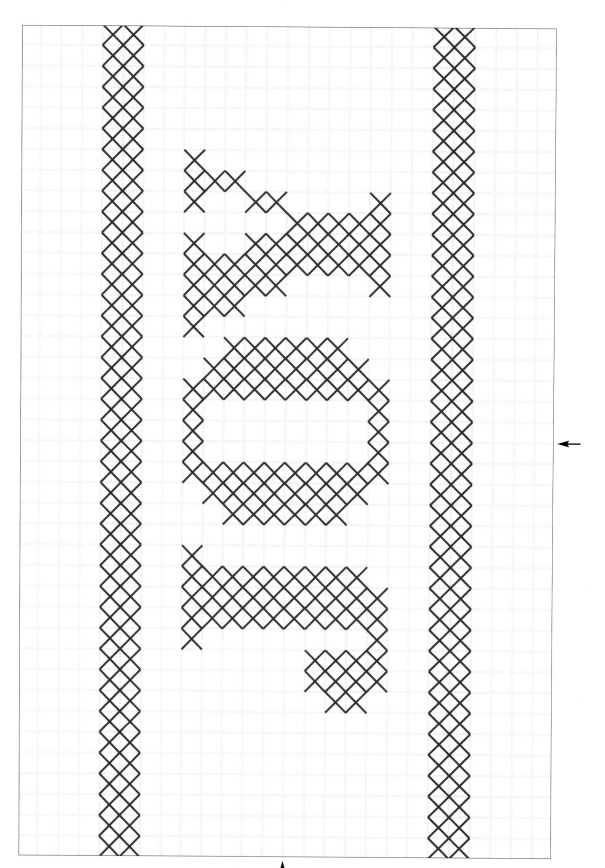

Beaded Castanets

Swirling patterns in this festive yarn's deeply saturated color bring to mind the sounds, rhythms, and hues of Spanish dance. The pillow is worked with two strands held together in Tunisian knit stitch. A trim of beaded picots adds a little *Olé!*

MEASUREMENTS

Finished size: 8 inches (20.3 centimeters) square, plus beaded trim

MATERIALS

Blue Heron Mercerized Cotton, 100% cotton, 8 ounces/227 grams, 1000 yards/914.4 meters

Spanish Dancer, 1 skein

Tunisian crochet hook size H, 5.0 mm or size needed to obtain gauge

Crochet hook size H, 5.0 mm or size that corresponds to Tunisian hook

Tapestry needle

Pillow form 8 inches (20.3 centimeters) square

Big-eye beading needle

Glass beads size 6/0, approximately 210

STITCHES AND ABBREVIATIONS

Chain stitch (ch)

Fasten off (fo)

RS (right side)

Single crochet (sc)

Skip (sk)

Slip stitch (sl st)

Stitch (st), stitches (sts)

Tunisian knit stitch (Tks)

Tunisian simple stitch (Tss)

WS (wrong side)

Yarn over (yo)

GAUGE

16 Tunisian stitches and 17 rows in Tunisian knit stitch/4 inches (10.2 centimeters)

For gauge swatch, using two strands held together, ch 20. Work in Tks pattern until swatch measures at least 4.5 inches (11.4 centimeters).

Special Stitches

Stringing beads

To string beads, use a big-eye beading needle.

Be careful: Both ends are quite sharp. Rather than holding the beads and trying to manipulate the needle into the hole, pour some beads onto a table or into a shallow dish and pick them up that way. When you are done with the needle, return it to its original packaging so nobody gets poked.

1. Put the yarn through the large eye of the beading needle.

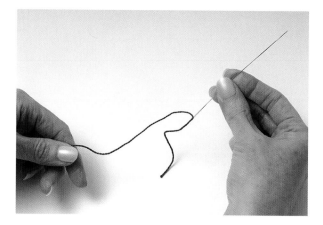

2. Use the end of the needle to pick up several beads.

3. Slide the beads past the needle onto the yarn.

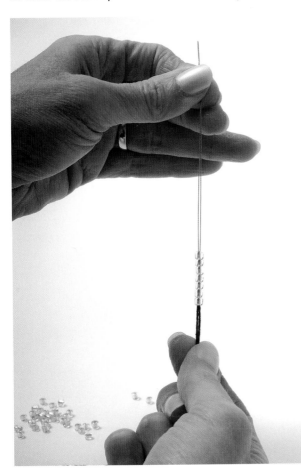

4. Push the beads down the yarn away from the needle, spreading them out as you go. You will slide them into position for the picots.

5. Remove needle.

Beaded Picot

1. Using yarn with beads already threaded on, ch 3.

2. Slide three beads up next to the hook.

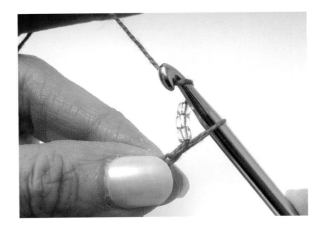

3. Ch 1 to hold beads in place.

4. Ch 3.

Pillow Top (Make 2)

Using 2 strands held together, ch 32.

Foundation row forward: Insert hook into second ch from hook, yo, pull up a lp. *Insert hook into next ch, yo, pull up a lp. Repeat from * across, adding 1 lp onto hook with each st. Total 32 lps on hook.

Foundation row return: Do not turn. Yo, pull through 1 lp. *Yo, pull through 2 lps. Repeat from * until 1 lp remains on hook.

> **NOTE** All return passes are worked this way.

Row 1: Sk first vertical bar. Tks in next st and in each st across to last st. Tss into final vertical bar and the horizontal bar behind it for stability. Return.

Repeat Row 1 until pillow measures 7 inches (17.8 centimeters).

Final row (switch to regular crochet hook if desired): Sk first vertical bar. *Insert hook in next st as for Tks. Yo, pull up lp, yo, pull through 2 lps (sc made). Repeat from * across to final st. Insert hook into vertical bar and horizontal thread behind it as for Tss. Yo, pull up lp, yo, pull through 2 lps (sc made). Continue working sc around remaining sides of pillow, working 2-3 sc in each corner. Join to first st with sl st. Fo.

Finishing and Assembly

With tapestry needle, weave in ends. Lightly steam block both pieces.

Position top and bottom with RS out, making sure the stitches are aligned the same way. Join two strands of yarn through both thicknesses (top and bottom of pillow). Using regular crochet hook, sc evenly around three sides, working 2-3 sc in each corner so the corner lies flat. Insert pillow form. Continue working sc along the fourth side to close pillow. Join to first st with sl st. Fo. Weave in ends.

Beaded Trim

> **NOTE** The trim uses only one strand of yarn, not two.

1. Using big eye beading needle, thread 210 beads onto one thickness of yarn.
2. Examine your pillow to decide which side looks "better." With the other side of the pillow facing you, join yarn to any corner of trim. The beaded picots will show better on the "good" side.
3. *Ch 3, slide three beads next to hook, ch 1 to hold beads in place, ch 3, sk 1 sc, sc in next sc. Repeat from * around perimeter of pillow, working final sc in place where you joined yarn. Fo. With tapestry needle, weave in end.
4. If necessary, lightly steam block the trim, being careful not to melt or crush the beads.

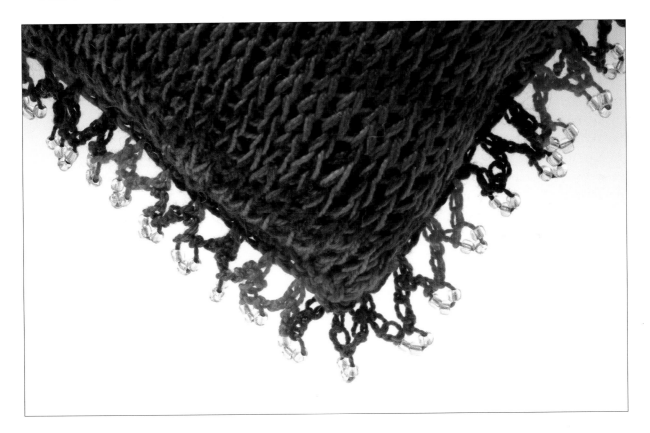

Royal Purple

This silk and merino wool yarn is luxuriously soft. Look closely at it, and you'll see the depth of the color. Along with several shades of purple there are also blues, indigo, and pink.

The Tunisian staggered X-stitch complements the yarn. The results are dramatic and elegant, fit for any throne.

MEASUREMENTS

Finished size: 11 inches (27.9 centimeters) square

MATERIALS

Plymouth Yarn Co. Mulberry Merino, 52% silk,
48% merino wool, 1.75 ounces/50 grams,
99 yards/90.5 meters

Color: Purple (454), 3 skeins

Tunisian hook size H, 5.0 mm or size needed to
obtain gauge

Crochet hook size H, 5.0 mm or size that corresponds
to Tunisian hook

Tapestry needle

Pillow form, 11 inches (27.9 centimeters) square

STITCHES AND ABBREVIATIONS

Chain stitch (ch)

Fasten off (fo)

Loop (lp), loops (lps)

Right side (RS)

Single crochet (sc)

Skip (sk)

Slip stitch (sl st)

Stitch (st), stitches (sts)

Tunisian simple stitch (Tss)

Yarn over (yo)

GAUGE

22 stitches and 15 rows in Tunisian staggered X-stitch
pattern/4 inches (10.2 centimeters)

NOTE Count the stitches individually, not in pairs.

For gauge swatch, ch 24 and work in pattern.

Special Stitches

Tunisian staggered X-stitch

Row 1 forward: Sk first vertical bar. The pattern is worked in pairs of stitches.

*Insert hook in *both* of next 2 vertical bars (keeping hook to the front of work).

Yo, pull up lp. Holding just-made lp in place with your index finger, insert hook in first vertical bar of the two bars just worked.

Yo, pull up lp. Sk second already-worked bar. Find the next pair of vertical bars. Repeat from * across to final vertical bar. Tss in final st, inserting hook into the vertical bar and the horizontal bar behind it for stability.

Row 1 return: Yo, pull through 1 lp. *Yo, pull through 2 lps. Repeat from * until 1 lp remains on hook.

NOTE All return passes are worked this way.

Row 2: Sk first vertical bar. Tss in next vertical bar. *Insert hook in next 2 vertical bars.

Yo, pull up lp. Holding just-made lp in place with your index finger, insert hook in first vertical bar of the two bars just worked, yo, pull up lp. Sk second already-worked bar. Find the next pair of vertical bars. Repeat from * across until 2 vertical bars remain. Tss into next vertical bar. Tss into final st, inserting hook into vertical bar and the horizontal bar behind it for stability.

Return.

Repeat Rows 1 and 2.

Pillow Top (Make 2)

Ch 50.

Foundation row forward: Insert hook in second ch from hook. Yo, pull up lp. 2 lps on hook. *Insert hook in next ch. Yo, pull up lp. Each st adds another lp to the hook. Repeat from * across. Total 50 lps on hook.

Return: Do not turn. Yo, pull through 1 lp. *Yo, pull through 2 lps. Repeat from * until 1 lp remains on hook.

NOTE All return passes are worked this way.

Work Rows 1 and 2 of pattern stitch until pillow top measures 9.5 inches (24.1 centimeters).

Final row (switch to regular crochet hook if desired): Sk first vertical bar. *Insert hook in next st as for Tss, yo, pull up lp, yo, pull through 2 lps (sc made). Repeat from * across top. Work 2-3 sc in the corner so it lays flat. Continue working sc around remaining sides of pillow, working 2-3 sc in each corner. Join to first st with sl st. Fo.

Finishing

Using tapestry needle, weave in ends. Gently steam block if desired.

Assembly

With RS out, position top and bottom of pillow. Join yarn through both thicknesses in any corner. Ch 1. Sc around three sides of pillow. Insert pillow form.

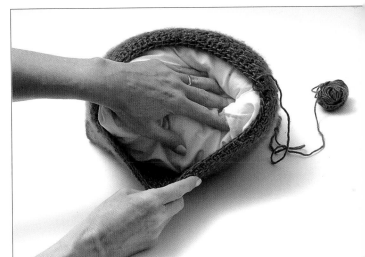

Close remaining side with sc.

Join to first st with sl st. Do not turn. Fo. Pull end to inside.

Santorini

SKILL LEVEL

EASY

Picture whitewashed buildings on the hillsides above the deep blues and greens of the Aegean Sea and you'll know why I named this pillow after a Greek island. Blocks of Tunisian simple stitch are arranged at right angles on the front; they are worked in one piece and joined as you go along. The back is worked in rows of single crochet. Front and back are joined with solid blue.

Toast yourself with a glass of *retsina* when you finish this project!

MEASUREMENTS

Finished size: 11 inches (27.9 centimeters) square

MATERIALS

S. Charles Collezione Nepal, 100% organic cotton, 1.75 ounces/50 grams, 98 yards/90 meters

Color A: 23 (blue and green), 3 skeins

Color B: 8 (cobalt), 1 skein

Tunisian hook size H, 5.0 mm or size needed to obtain gauge

Crochet hook size H, 5.0 mm or size that corresponds to Tunisian hook

Tapestry needle

Pillow form, 11 inches square (27.9 centimeters)

STITCHES AND ABBREVIATIONS

Chain stitch (ch)

Fasten off (fo)

Loop (lp), loops (lps)

Right side (RS)

Single crochet (sc)

Skip (sk)

Slip stitch (sl st)

Stitch (st), stitches (sts)

Tunisian simple stitch (Tss)

Wrong side (WS)

Yarn over (yo)

GAUGE

16 stitches and 16 rows in Tunisian simple stitch/4 inches (10.2 centimeters). For gauge swatch, ch 20 and work in Tss.

NOTE If your gauge is correct, you can use your swatch to start the first block on the front.

Pillow Front

Block 1

With A, ch 20.

Foundation row forward: Insert hook in second ch from hook. Yo, pull up lp. 2 lps on hook. *Insert hook in next ch. Yo, pull up lp. Each st adds another lp to the hook. Repeat from * across. Total 20 lps on hook.

Return: Do not turn. Yo, pull through 1 lp. *Yo, pull through 2 lps. Repeat from * until 1 lp remains on hook.

NOTE All return passes are worked this way.

Row 1 forward: Sk first vertical bar. Tss in each vertical bar across to final st. Insert hook into vertical bar and the horizontal bar behind it for stability. Yo, pull up lp. 20 lps on hook.

Row 1 return: Yo, pull through 1 lp. *Yo, pull through 2 lps. Repeat from * until 1 lp remains on hook.

Rows 2-18: Repeat Row 1.

Row 19: Sk first vertical bar. *Insert hook in next vertical bar, yo, pull up lp, yo, pull through 2 lps (sc made). Repeat from * across. This gives 20 rows including the foundation row. Do not fo.

Block 2

Row 1: Rotate Block 1 ninety degrees. Ch 1. Tss in ends of rows from previous block, which are now at the top of your work. The sts you make will be perpendicular to the ones on Block 1. Total 20 lps on hook. Return.

Row 2: Sk first vertical bar. Tss in each vertical bar across. Return.

Rows 3-19: Repeat row 2.

Row 20: Sk first vertical bar. *Insert hook in next vertical bar, yo, pull up lp, yo, pull through 2 lps (sc made). Repeat from * across. Do not fo.

Block 3

Repeat Block 2

Block 4

Row 1: Turn blocks ninety degrees. Ch 1. Tss in each st across. For final st, put hook through from front to back and also go through end of Block 1 to join the blocks together. Return normally.

Row 2: Sk first vertical bar. Tss in each st across. For final st, put hook through from front to back and also go through end of Block 1 to join blocks together. Return.

Rows 3-19: Repeat Row 2.

Row 20: Sk first vertical bar. *Insert hook in next vertical bar, yo, pull up lp, yo, pull through 2 lps (sc made). Repeat from * across. Repeat from * across, joining to Block 1 with final st. Fo.

Trim for Front

NOTE You may use a regular crochet hook.

Row 1: With RS facing, join B in any corner. Ch 1. Sc in each st or end of row around, working 2-3 sc in each corner so it lays flat. Join with sl st to first st. Turn.

Row 2: Ch 1. Sc in each sc around. Join to first st with sl st.

Row 3: Repeat Row 2. Fo.

Back

NOTE You may use a regular crochet hook.

Row 1: With A, ch 34. Sc in second ch from hook and in each ch across. Total 33 sc. Turn.

Row 2: Ch 1. Sc in each sc across.

Repeat Row 2 until back measures 10 inches (25.4 centimeters), ending with WS row. Fo.

Trim for Back

Round 1: With RS facing, join B in corner of back where you left off. Ch 1. Sc across row and evenly all around the square, working 2 or 3 sc in each corner so piece lies flat. Join to first st with sl st. Turn.

Round 2: Ch 1. Turn. Sc in each st around, working 2 or 3 sc in each corner so piece lies flat. Join to first st with sl st.

Round 3: Repeat Round 2.

Rounds 4-7: Repeat Round 2 but do not work extra sts in the corners. You want those to bend upward to create a box shape. Fo.

Finishing

Using tapestry needle, weave in ends. Lightly steam block if desired.

Assembly

Put top and bottom together, WS out. Join yarn through both thicknesses in any corner. Sc top trim to bottom around three sides. Fo.

Turn RS out. Insert pillow form. Cut a few yards of B. Thread tapestry needle. Sew remaining side closed. Cut thread. Pull excess through to inside of pillow.

Debonair

SKILL LEVEL

INTERMEDIATE

This sophisticated black and white pillow is classic but not stodgy thanks to three contemporary black buttons. Tunisian net stitch, worked in the spaces between stitches, is quick and easy and creates a unique woven look.

The pillow is constructed in three pieces: a solid black back and a two-part white front that overlaps and closes with chain loops around the buttons.

MEASUREMENTS

Finished size: 11 inches (27.9 centimeters) square

MATERIALS

Louet Gems #2 fine/sport weight 100% merino wool, 100 grams/3.5 ounces, 225 yards/205 meters

Color A: White (80/2703-18/8), 1 skein

Color B: Black (80/2223-29/9), 1 skein

Tunisian hook size H, 5.0 mm or size needed to obtain gauge

Crochet hook size H, 5.0 mm or size that corresponds to Tunisian hook

Tapestry needle

Three decorative buttons, approximately 1.5 to 2 inches (3.8 to 5.1 centimeters) across widest dimension

Black sewing thread

Sewing needle

Stitch markers

Pillow form, 11 inches (27.9 centimeters) square

STITCHES AND ABBREVIATIONS

Chain stitch (ch)

Fasten off (fo)

Loop (lp), loops (lps)

Right side (RS)

Single crochet (sc)

Skip (sk)

Stitch (st), stitches (sts)

Tunisian net stitch (Tns)

Tunisian simple stitch (Tss)

Yo (yarn over)

GAUGE

20 sts and 25 rows in Tunisian net stitch/4 inches (10.2 centimeters). For gauge swatch, ch 25 and work in Tns until swatch measures 4.5 inches (11.4 centimeters).

> **NOTE** The rows are staggered. When testing gauge, be sure to count every row, not every other row.

Special Stitch

Tunisian net stitch

Start with the basic forward and return in Tss.

Row 1: Sk first 2 vertical bars. Tss into space between second and third sts, poking hook from front to back. Tss into each sp to final vertical bar. Tss into final vertical bar and horizontal bar behind it for stability. Return.

The photo shows the space between sts.

Row 2: Sk first vertical bar. Tss into space between first and second vertical bars. Tss into each sp to last sp. Sk that last sp. Tss into final vertical bar and horizontal bar behind it for stability. Return.

The photo shows how the sts are staggered between each other from one row to the next.

Repeat Rows 1 and 2 for pattern.

NOTE To keep the same number of lps on the hook while creating the staggered net pattern, skip the first space at the beginning of one row and do not skip any spaces at the far end of that row. You may have to look closely to find that last space. On the next row, work into the first space but skip the last space at the far end. Count your stitches to make sure you have the correct number.

Pillow Front, Main Piece

With A, ch 57.

Foundation row forward: Insert hook in second ch from hook. Yo, pull up lp. *Insert hook in next ch. Yo, pull up lp. Each st adds another lp to the hook. Repeat from * across. Total 57 lps on hook.

Foundation row return: Do not turn. Yo, pull through 1 lp. *Yo, pull through 2 lps. Repeat from * until 1 lp remains on hook.

NOTE All return passes are worked this way.

Row 1: Sk first 2 vertical bars. Tns into space between second and third sts by putting hook from front to back through that sp, yo, pull to front.

NOTE Make sure you are working between two sts, not within a st.

*Tns into next sp. Repeat from * across, working Tns into final sp and Tss into final vertical bar and the horizontal bar behind it for stability. Total 57 lps on hook. Return.

Row 2: Sk first vertical bar. *Tns into next sp. Repeat from * across until 1 sp remains. Sk final sp. Tss into final vertical bar and the horizontal bar behind it for stability. Total 57 lps on hook. Return.

Repeat Rows 1 and 2 until fabric measures 9.5 inches (42.1 centimeters). When 2 sts remain on hook, switch to B.

Final row (contrasting color border; you may use regular crochet hook if desired): Insert hook in space as for Tns, yo, pull to front, yo pull through 2 lps (sc made). Continue across, working 2-3 sc in corner so piece lies flat. Sc evenly around remaining three sides. Join to first st with sl st. Fo.

Pillow Front, Small Piece

Work as for main piece of front until fabric measures 3.5 inches (8.9 centimeters). Work final row in contrasting color as for main piece.

Pillow Back

Using B, work as for main piece of front until fabric measures 10 inches (25.4 centimeters). Do not switch colors for the final row.

Finishing

With tapestry needle, weave in ends. Lightly steam block pieces.

Assembly

With RS out, arrange large front piece on top of back. Join B at top of front piece (does not correspond to top of back) through both thicknesses. Sc evenly down side, across bottom, and up other side. Fo.

Now arrange small front piece over large front piece so the top of the small front piece is even with the top of the back piece. The edge of the top piece should overlap the top edge of the bottom piece. Join yarn at bottom of front piece; you will have to go through the top and the two thicknesses that are already together for a few stitches. Sc around to other edge. Fo.

Position buttons evenly across front of main piece, approximately 5-6 inches (12.7-15.2 centimeters) down from top of pillow. With black thread, sew in place.

Mark corresponding spots for ch lps. Join B in each spot. Ch 12, join with sl st to place where you joined yarn. Fo.

NOTE Test the length of the ch lps as you go along. They should be long enough to slip over the buttons and hold the pillow closed without strain. Adjust the number of chs if necessary.

Weave in ends. Insert pillow form.

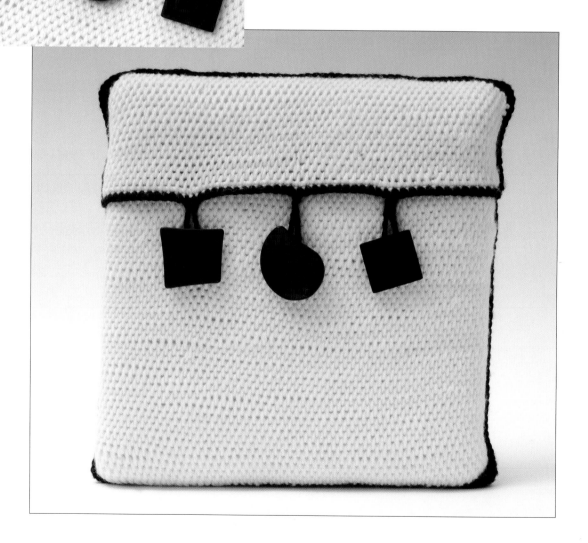

Sweet Dreams

SKILL LEVEL

INTERMEDIATE

This sweet little pillow combines Tunisian crossed stitches with Tunisian knit stitches for texture and visual interest. Picot trim adds just the right finishing touch.

The yarn is machine washable, making this pillow practical as well as beautiful. Give it for a shower or new baby gift that will be treasured for years.

MEASUREMENTS

Finished size: 12 inches (30.5 centimeters) wide by 8 inches (20.3 centimeters) high plus picot trim

MATERIALS

Plymouth Yarn Co. Dreambaby Shine, 45% acrylic microfiber, 45% nylon, 10% rayon, 1.75 ounces/ 50 grams, 160 yards/146.3 meters

Color: Pale mint green (105), 2 skeins

Tunisian hook size H, 5.0 mm or size needed to obtain gauge

Crochet hook size H, 5.0 mm or size that corresponds to Tunisian hook

Tapestry needle

Pillow form, 8 by 12 inches (20.3 by 30.5 centimeters)

STITCHES AND ABBREVIATIONS

Chain stitch (ch)

Fasten off (fo)

Loop (lp), loops (lps)

Right side (RS)

Single crochet (sc)

Skip (sk)

Slip stitch (sl)

Stitch (st), stitches (sts)

Tunisian knit stitch (Tks)

Tunisian simple stitch (Tss)

Wrong side (WS)

Yarn over (yo)

GAUGE

18 stitches and 16 rows in pattern/4 inches (10 centimeters)

For gauge swatch, ch 24. Insert hook in second ch from hook, yo, pull up lp. *Insert hook in next ch, yo, pull up lp. Repeat from * across. Total 24 lps on hook. To return, yo, pull through 1 lp, *yo, pull through 2 lps. Repeat from * until 1 lp remains on hook.

Work in Tunisian cross pattern until swatch measures at least 4.5 inches (11.4 centimeters)

Special Stitches

Tunisian cross pattern

The 4-row pattern alternates 2 rows of crossed Tunisian simple stitches with 2 rows of Tunisian knit stitches.

Row 1 forward: Every pair of sts, except for the first st and the last st, is worked in an X shape.

NOTE The photo shows the second and third vertical bars (the first one is all the way to the right). In the marked pair, you will work the far one first, then return for the one you skipped. As always, the first vertical bar on the row remains unworked.

Skip first 2 vertical bars, Tss in next vertical bar.

Working in front of st just made, Tss in the second skipped vertical bar (the one immediately before the one where you just made the Tss). To make it easier to find the skipped vertical bar, gently stretch the work.

*Move to next pair of unworked vertical bars. Sk next vertical bar, Tss in following vertical bar. Working in front of st just made, Tss in skipped vertical bar. Repeat from * to last vertical bar. Tss in last vertical bar (also picking up the horizontal strand immediately behind it for stability). Do not turn.

Row 1 return: Yo, pull through 1 lp. *Yo, pull through 2 lps. Repeat from * until 1 lp remains on hook.

NOTE All subsequent return rows are worked this way.

Row 2 forward and return: Repeat Row 1. The crossed pairs of stitches will now be crossed again.

Row 3: Sk first vertical bar. Tks in each st across to last st.

Tss in final st. Return.

Row 4: Repeat Row 3.

NOTE The swatch above shows two rows of Tks at the top. (There are several rows of X-stitches; your pattern will use 2 X-stitch rows followed by 2 Tks rows.)

Pillow Front

Ch 50.

Foundation row forward: Insert hook in second ch from hook. Yo, pull up lp. *Insert hook in next ch. Yo, pull up lp. Each st adds another lp to the hook. Repeat from * across. Total 50 lps on hook.

Return: Do not turn. Yo, pull through 1 lp. *Yo, pull through 2 lps. Repeat from * until 1 lp remains on hook.

Row 2: Sk first vertical bar. Tks in each st across to last st; Tss in final st. Return.

Rows 3–6: Work in stitch pattern. The back (WS) will begin to show a series of ridges.

Repeat Rows 3–6 until pillow front measures 6 inches.

Repeat Rows 3–5 once more.

Final row (finishes pillow and starts edging; switch to regular crochet hook if desired): Sk first vertical bar. *Insert hook into next vertical bar as for Tks. Yo, pull up lp, yo, pull through 2 lps (sc made). Repeat from * across, then sc evenly down side, across bottom, and up other side, working 2-3 sc in each corner so that piece lies flat. Join to first st with sl st. Fo.

Back (Make 2)

> **NOTE** The back is worked in two pieces that overlap when assembled.

Ch 50.

Foundation row: Insert hook in second ch from hook, yo, pull up lp. *Insert hook in next ch, yo, pull up lp. Repeat from * across. Total 50 lps on hook. Return.

Rows 1-21: Sk first vertical bar. Tks in next vertical bar and in each st across to final vertical bar. Tss in final vertical bar. Return.

Row 22 (switch to regular crochet hook if desired): Sk first vertical bar. *Insert hook into next vertical bar as for Tks. Yo, pull up lp, yo, pull through 2 lps (sc made). Repeat from * across, then sc evenly down side, across bottom, and up other side, working 2-3 sc in each corner so that piece lies flat. Join to first st with sl st. Fo.

Finishing

With tapestry needle, weave in ends. Gently steam block if desired.

Assembly

With RS out, arrange front with top back piece in place.

Join yarn where the bottom of that top back piece meets the front. Sc through both thicknesses up short side, across top, and down other short side. Fo.

The second piece of the back will overlap the first piece you just attached. With RS out, arrange it in place. Attach yarn at top of that bottom piece. Sc through both thicknesses (will be 3 layers thick for first few sts) down short side, across bottom, and up other short side. Fo.

Weave in ends. Insert pillow form.

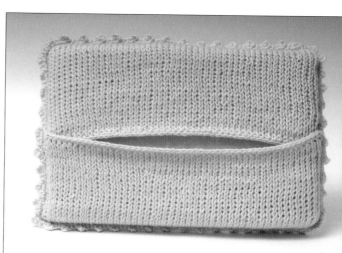

> **NOTE** The photo shows how the back pieces fit together. Once the pillow form is enclosed, the pieces overlap so the form does not show.

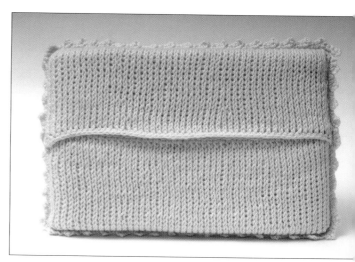

Picot Trim

With front facing you, join yarn in any corner. Ch 1. *Sc in each of next 3 sc. Ch 3. Sl st into top of sc at base of chs to complete picot.

Repeat from * around all 4 sides. Join to first sc with sl st. Fo.

Honeycomb Bolster

Tunisian honeycomb stitch, which alternates Tunisian purl stitches and Tunisian simple stitches, is a fancy-looking but simply executed pattern that really shows off variegated yarn. The body of the bolster is worked first; a circle of single crochet on each end closes the cylinder.

MEASUREMENTS

Finished size: 13 inches (33 centimeters) long,
6 inches (15.2 centimeters) in diameter

MATERIALS

Kangaroo Dyer 75% superwash wool (25% nylon),
450 yards

Color: 1 (Beach Towel), 1 skein

Tunisian hook size H, 5.0 mm or size needed to
obtain gauge

Crochet hook size H, 5.0 mm or size that corresponds
to Tunisian hook

Stitch marker

Tapestry needle

Straight pins

Bolster pillow form, 13 inches (33 centimeters) long,
6 inches (15.2 centimeters) in diameter

STITCHES AND ABBREVIATIONS

Chain stitch (ch)

Fasten off (fo)

Loop (lp), loops (lps)

Right side (RS)

Single crochet (sc)

Stitch (st), stitches (sts)

Tunisian purl stitch (Tps)

Tunisian simple stitch (Tss)

Yo (yarn over)

GAUGE

12 honeycomb sts (each honeycomb st equals Tps,
Tss) and 15 honeycomb rows/4 inches (10.2
centimeters)

NOTE For stitches, count in pairs. Count rows individually.

For gauge swatch, ch 31 and work in pattern.

Special Stitches

Tunisian honeycomb stitch

Row 1: Sk first vertical bar. *Tps in next st, Tss in next st.
Repeat from * across to last st. Work Tss into final vertical
bar and horizontal bar behind it for stability.

For the Tunisian purl stitch, bring the yarn in front of the
hook:

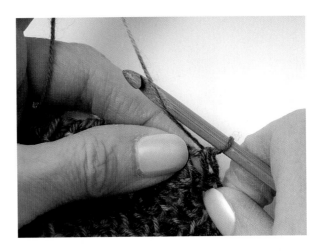

Insert hook into next bar.

Bring yarn in front of bar and down behind hook.

Yo, pull up lp to complete the st.

The next st is a Tss. The photo shows the unworked vertical bar on the far right, a Tps (identifiable by the yarn crossing in front), and a Tss.

To return, yo, pull through 1 lp. *Yo, pull through 2 lps. Repeat from * until 1 lp remains on hook.

NOTE All return passes are worked this way.

Row 2: Sk first vertical bar. *Tss in next st, Tps in next st.

NOTE You will be working Tss into Tps, and Tps into Tss.

Repeat from * across to last st. Work Tss into final vertical bar and horizontal bar behind it for stability. Return. Repeat Rows 1 and 2.

Here is what the fabric looks like after several rows. Note that the stitches are staggered (Tps over Tss, Tss over Tps) to create the honeycomb effect.

Pillow

Ch 75.

Foundation row forward: Insert hook in second ch from hook. Yo, pull up lp. *Insert hook in next ch. Yo, pull up lp. Each st adds another lp to the hook. Repeat from * across. Total 75 lps on hook.

Foundation row return: Do not turn. Yo, pull through 1 lp. *Yo, pull through 2 lps. Repeat from * until 1 lp remains on hook.

> **NOTE** All return passes are worked this way.

Row 1: Sk first vertical bar. *Tps in next vertical bar, Tss in next vertical bar. Repeat from * across to final vertical bar. Tss in final vertical bar and horizontal bar behind it for stability. Total 75 lps on hook. Return.

> **NOTE** The final stitch on every row is a Tss.

Row 2: Sk first vertical bar. *Tss in next st, Tps in next st. Return.

> **NOTE** You are working Tss into Tps from previous row, and Tps into Tss from previous row.

Repeat Rows 1 and 2 until pillow measures approximately 18.5 inches (47 centimeters), ending with Row 2. Do not fo.

Final row (switch to regular crochet hook if desired): Sk first vertical bar. *Insert hook into next st as for Tps, yo, pull up lp, yo, pull through 2 lps (sc made). Insert hook into next st as for Tss, yo, pull up lp, yo, pull through 2 lps (sc made). Repeat from * until final st. Insert hook in stitch as for Tss into vertical bar and horizontal thread behind it. Yo, pull up lp, yo, pull through 2 lps. Do not fo. Insert stitch marker in loop to keep work from unraveling during blocking.

Close Pillow

With tapestry needle, weave in ends. Gently steam block. Arrange pillow into a tube with RS inside. Working through both thicknesses, sc in each st across to close pillow across its length. Fo.

Pillow Ends (Make 2)

> **NOTE** After you ch 1 to start each new round, place a stitch marker in that ch. It will help you identify where the new round starts so you know where to join with a sl st.

With regular crochet hook, ch 3. Sl st into first ch to form ring.

Round 1: Ch 1. Work 8 sc in ring. Sl st into first st to join.

Round 2: Ch 1. Work 2 sc into each sc around. Sl st into first st to join. Total 16 sc.

Round 3: Ch 1. *Sc in next sc, 2 sc in next sc. Repeat from * around. Sl st into first st to join. Total 24 sc.

Round 4: Ch 1. *Sc in each of next 2 sc, 2 sc in next sc. Repeat from * around. Sl st into first st to join. Total 32 sc.

Round 5: Ch 1. *Sc in each of next 3 sc, 2 sc in next sc. Repeat from * around. Sl st into first st to join. Total 40 sc.

Round 6: Ch 1. *Sc in each of next 4 sc, 2 sc in next sc. Repeat from * around. Sl st into first st to join. Total 48 sc.

Round 7: Ch 1. *Sc in each of next 5 sc, 2 sc in next sc. Repeat from * around. Sl st into first st to join. Total 56 sc.

Round 8: Ch 1. Sc in each sc around. Sl st into first st to join. Total 56 sc.

Round 9: Repeat Round 8.

Round 10: Ch 1. *Sc in each of next 6 sc, 2 sc in next sc. Repeat from * around. Sl st into first st to join. Total 64 sc.

Round 11. Ch 1. Sc in each sc around. Sl st into first st to join. Total 64 sc.

Round 12: Ch 1. *Sc in each of next 7 sc, 2 sc in next sc. Repeat from * around. Sl st into first st to join. Total 72 sc.

Round 13: Ch 1. *Sc in each of next 8 sc, 2 sc in next sc. Repeat from * around. Sl st into first st to join. Total 80 sc.

Round 14: Ch 1. Sc in each sc around. Sl st into first st to join. Total 80 sc.

Round 15. Ch 1. *Sc in each of next 9 sc, 2 sc in next sc. Repeat from * around. Sl st into first st to join. Total 88 sc.

> **NOTE** After each subsequent round, measure your circle against the end of the pillow form. Stop crocheting when your circle is about a half-inch to 1 inch smaller in diameter than the end of the pillow form. You may not need all 19 rounds.

Round 16: Ch 1. Sc in each sc around. Sl st into first st to join. Total 88 sc.

Round 17: Ch 1. *Sc in each of next 10 sc, 2 sc in next sc. Repeat from * around. Sl st into first st to join. Total 96 sc.

Round 18. Ch 1. *Sc in each of next 11 sc, 2 sc in next sc. Repeat from * around. Sl st into first st to join. Total 104 sc.

Round 19: Ch 1. Sc in each st around. Sl st into first st to join. Total 104 sc. Fo.

Finishing

Using tapestry needle, weave in ends, using the starting thread in the center to help pull the initial ring closed. Gently steam block pieces.

Assembly

Turn body of pillow RS out. Place one pillow end in place, RS out. Pin to the main section. Attach yarn in any spot. Ch 1. Working through both thicknesses, sc evenly around, removing pins as you get to them. This creates a neat ridge along the edge. Sl st to first st to join. Fo.

Insert pillow form. Repeat assembly on other pillow end. Pull yarn ends to inside of pillow.

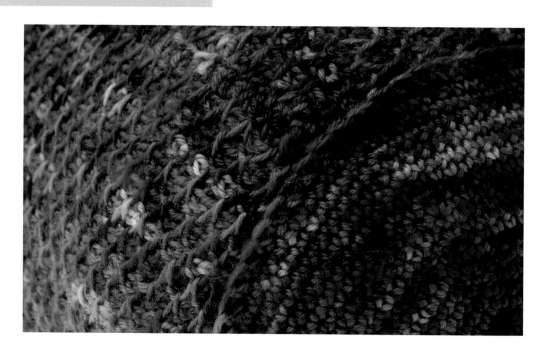

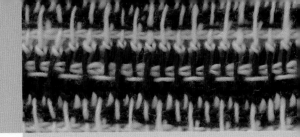

Café au Lait

SKILL LEVEL

■■■▢
INTERMEDIATE

Rich shades of cream and brown in delicate baby merino lace are worked in a "dots-and-dashes" Tunisian stitch pattern to give this small pillow a big impact. The more you look at it, the more you'll see: horizontal strands moving across a row in front of and behind vertical bars, tiny V shapes poking in and out, tall vertical bars alternating with shorter ones, interesting color contrasts. Drink it all in and enjoy.

MEASUREMENTS

Finished size: 9 inches (22.9 centimeters) square

MATERIALS

Abuelita Baby Merino Lace, 100% merino wool,
   3.5 ounces/100 grams, 420 yards/384 meters

Color A: Chocolate brown (60B2), 1 skein

Color B: Raw white (3), 1 skein

Color C: Desert flower (69M8), 1 skein

Tunisian hook size H, 5.00 mm or size needed
   to obtain gauge

Crochet hook size H, 5.00 mm or size that
   corresponds to Tunisian hook

Tapestry needle

Pillow form 9 inches (22.9 centimeters) square

STITCHES AND ABBREVIATIONS

Chain stitch (ch)

Fasten off (fo)

Loop (lp), loops (lps)

Right side (RS)

Single crochet (sc)

Slip stitch (sl st)

Stitch (st), stitches (sts)

Tunisian extended stitch (Tes)

Tunisian simple stitch (Tss)

Yo (yarn over)

GAUGE

19 sts and 13 rows in pattern/4 inches (10.2
   centimeters)

> **NOTE** The weaving row and the Tunisian extended stitch row are not the same heights; make sure to count the rows correctly when measuring gauge. It's easiest to do this in sets of two rows.

For gauge swatch, ch 23 and work in pattern until swatch measures 4.5 inches (11.4 centimeters).

Special Stitches

Tunisian extended stitch

Insert hook where indicated in pattern. Yo, pull up lp, ch 1. (This is the same as a Tunisian simple stitch with a chain stitch added onto the end.)

Pillow Top (Make 2)

Foundation row (RS): With A, ch 49. Pull up lp in second ch from hook and in each ch across. Total 49 lps.

Foundation row return: Do not turn. Yo, pull through 1 lp, *yo, pull through 2 lps. Repeat from * across, changing to B when 2 lps remain on hook. Do not cut A, just carry it up the side along the end of the rows.

Row 1: Sk first vertical bar. Slide next vertical bar on hook; do not pull up a lp, just put the hook through, keeping the hook to the front. *Bring yarn to the front of your work, slip next vertical bar on hook, move yarn to the back of the work, slip next vertical bar on hook. Repeat from * across to final vertical bar. Total 49 lps on hook. Return.

The photos show how the yarn is brought to the front and the back of the stitches but not pulled up.

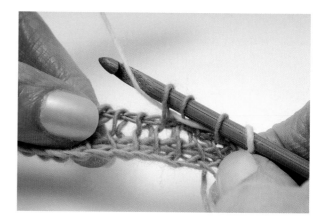

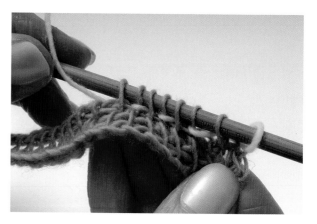

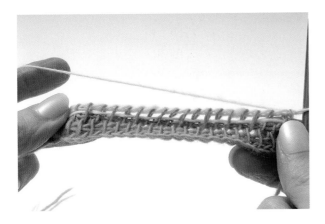

Notice that on this row, the yarn is brought to the front of the work before a vertical bar is slipped onto the hook.

Row 2: Sk first vertical bar. Ch 1. Tes in each st across. Return, changing to A when 2 lps remain on hook. Do not cut B.

The photo below shows the end of the forward pass on the Tes row.

Here you can see that the horizontal strands are staggered: the lower one comes to the front when the upper one is in the back, and vice versa.

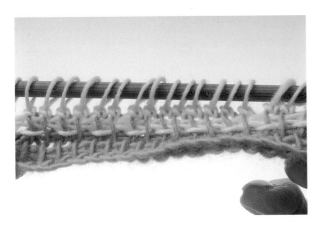

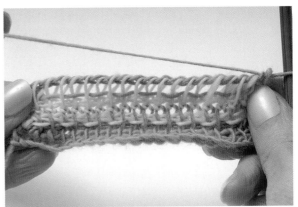

Row 3: Sk first vertical bar. Bring yarn to front of work. Working behind yarn, slip next vertical bar on hook. *Bring yarn to back of work. Working in front of yarn, slip next vertical bar on hook. Bring yarn to front of work; working behind yarn, sl next vertical bar on hook. Repeat from * across to last vertical bar. Return.

Row 4: Repeat Row 2, changing to A when 2 lps remain on hook.

Repeat Rows 1-4 twice, then rows 1-2 once more. Change to C when 2 lps remain on hook. Cut B, leaving 4-inch tail. You will attach a new strand of B when called for in the pattern.

With colors A and C, repeat Rows 1-4 three times, then rows 1-2 once more. Change to B when 2 lps remain on hook. Cut C.

With colors A and B, repeat Rows 1-4 three times, then Row 1 once more.

Final row (may use regular crochet hook if desired): Sk first vertical bar. With A, insert hook in next vertical bar as for Tss. Yo, pull to front, yo, pull through 2 (sc made). Sc in each st across, working 2-3 sc in each corner so it lies flat. Continue working sc all the way around. Join to first st with sl st. Fo.

Finishing

With tapestry needle, weave in ends. Gently steam block.

Assembly

Position pillow front and back with RS out. Using A, join yarn in any corner through both thicknesses (use regular crochet hook if desired). Sc around three sides of pillow. Insert form. Close remaining side with sc. Join to first st with sl st. Fo. Pull end of yarn to inside of pillow.

Techniques

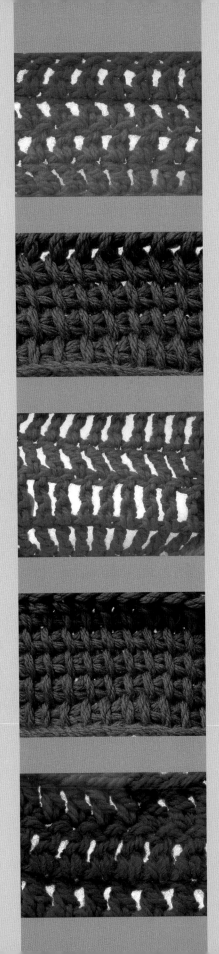

Traditional Crochet

In traditional crochet—the style most people are familiar with—only one stitch at a time is active. Each is worked to completion before the next stitch is begun. Stitch heights progress from the low-profile slip stitch through single crochet, half double crochet, double crochet, treble crochet, and beyond, based on how many times the yarn is wrapped around the hook and how the loops are pulled through other loops. Hooks for traditional crochet are usually 5–8 inches long and can be made of metal, plastic, bamboo, wood, or other materials.

Chain Stitch

1. Attach yarn to hook with slip knot. Yarn over, pull through.

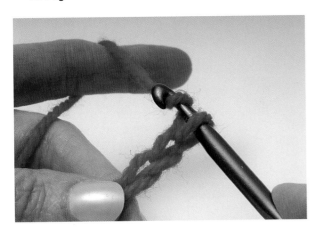

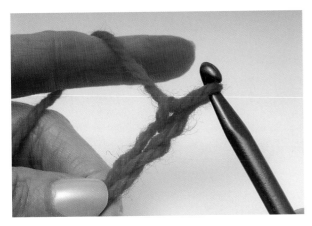

Slip Stitch

1. Insert hook into work where instructed. (This stitch is often used to close a ring.)

2. Yarn over, pull through both loops.

Single Crochet

3. Yarn over, pull through both loops.

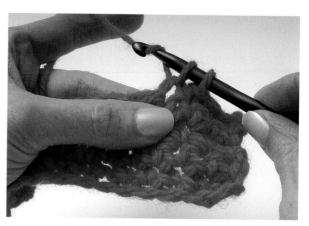

1. Insert hook into work where instructed. If you are working into the foundation chain, this will be the second chain from the hook.

2. Yarn over, pull up a loop.

Half Double Crochet

1. Yarn over.

2. Insert hook into work where instructed. If you are working into the foundation chain, this will be the third chain from the hook.

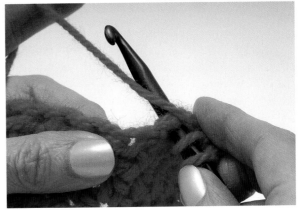

3. Yarn over, pull up a loop.

4. Yarn over, pull through all three loops.

Double Crochet

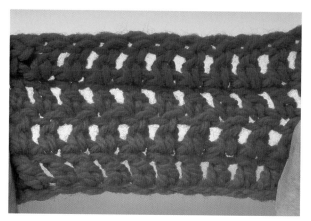

1. Yarn over.

2. Insert hook into the work where instructed. If you are working into the foundation chain, this will be the fourth chain from the hook.

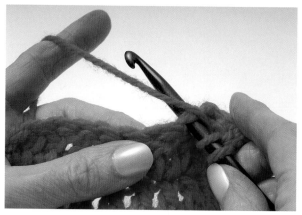

3. Yarn over, pull up a loop.

4. Yarn over, pull through two loops.

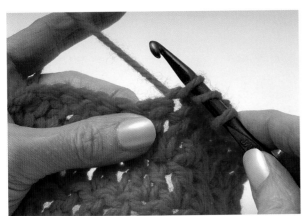

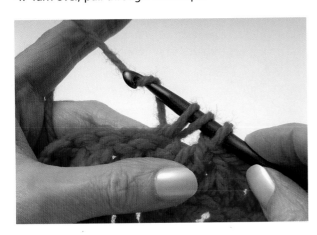

5. Yarn over, pull through remaining two loops.

Treble Crochet

3. Yarn over, pull up a loop.

1. Yarn over twice.

2. Insert hook into the work where instructed. If you are working into the foundation chain, this will be the fifth chain from the hook.

4. Yarn over, pull through two loops.

6. Yarn over, pull through remaining two loops.

5. Yarn over, pull through two loops.

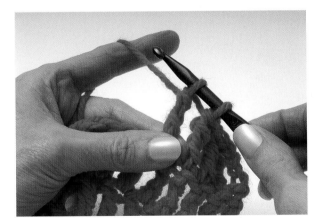

Change Colors or Start a New Skein

1. Work in pattern as indicated. The photo shows double crochet fabric.

2. Work the next stitch until two loops remain on hook, no matter what type of stitch it is.

3. Drop the current yarn to the back. Yarn over with the new color and complete the stitch.

4. Continue to work with new yarn.

Tunisian Crochet

Tunisian crochet, also known as the "afghan stitch," combines aspects of crocheting and knitting. Like crocheting, it uses a hook and the same hand motions used in traditional crochet; as in knitting, loops are added to the hook so there are many active stitches at once. Tunisian crochet uses either a long hook with a stopper on the end or a shorter hook with a plastic extension to accommodate the many loops that will be on the hook at one time. Tunisian fabric can look knitted, woven, or textured, and lacks the "loopy" appearance of traditional crochet.

The photo shows a ChiaoGoo bamboo hook with a flexible extension and bead stopper.

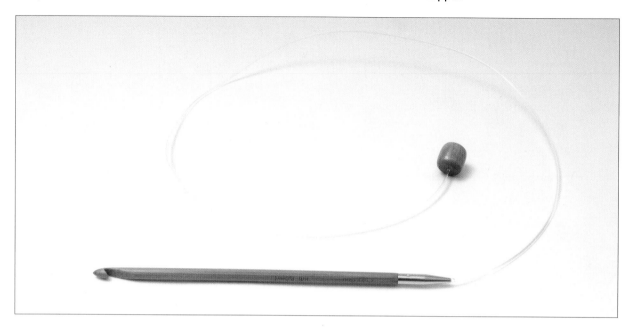

Here is a set of versatile Denise Interchangeable Crochet Hooks.
Different size hooks can be attached to different lengths of plastic cord.

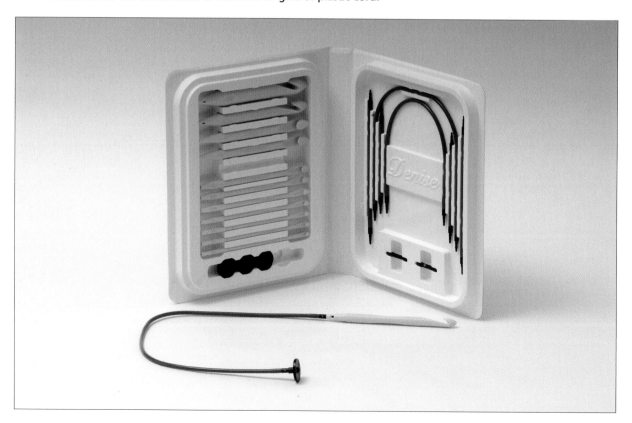

Foundation Row

> **NOTE** All Tunisian fabrics start with this basic row.

Foundation Row Forward

1. Make the number of chain stitches indicated in the pattern.

> **NOTE** The number of Tunisian stitches on subsequent rows will be the same as the number of chains you start with.

2. Insert hook in second chain from hook. Yarn over, pull up loop. There will be two loops on the hook.

> **NOTE** To minimize the curl in Tunisian crochet, you could work into the back bump of the chain. I usually put the stitches in the regular place, not the back bump, and rely on steam blocking to eliminate the curl.

3. Hook in the next chain. Yarn over, pull up loop. Each stitch adds another loop to the hook.

4. Continue in this fashion all the way across.

5. Count the loops. You should have the same number of loops on the hook as the number of foundation chains.

Foundation Row Return

1. Yarn over, pull through one loop.

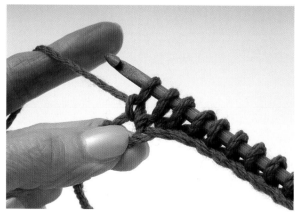

2. Yarn over, pull through two loops.

3. Repeat Step 2 all the way across until one loop remains on the hook.

> **NOTE** This return method is referred to as the "standard return." Follow this procedure for the return pass unless instructed otherwise.

Tunisian Simple Stitch

Work foundation row forward and return. Look at the finished stitches. You will see a vertical bar for each stitch. These bars are what you will work behind as you make the Tunisian simple stitch forward pass.

1. Skip the first vertical bar that is on the far right side, directly below the hook.

2. Put the hook from right to left through the next vertical bar. Keep the hook to the front of the work. Yarn over, pull up a loop. There will be two loops on the hook.

3. Repeat Step 2 in each stitch across (except for the far left bar), adding a loop to the hook with each stitch.

4. To work the final stitch, identify the final vertical bar and the horizontal thread that runs behind it. Insert the hook so it is behind both of these threads. When viewed from the side, the two threads look like a backwards *6* for right-handers and a regular *6* for lefties.

Yarn over, pull up a loop. Count the loops. You should have the same number as you did on the foundation row.

5. Work standard return.

The photo below shows Tunisian simple stitch fabric.

Tunisian Knit Stitch

Work foundation row forward and return. Look at the finished stitches. Each stitch has two "legs" in an upside-down V shape. Instead of keeping the hook to the front like you did in Tunisian simple stitch, for Tunisian knit stitch you will poke the hook from front to back through the center of each stitch.

Forward Pass

1. Skip the first vertical bar that is on the far right side, directly below the hook.
2. Put the hook from front to back through the next stitch. (Stretch the stitch out slightly to see where the two vertical legs are; go right between them, not between two stitches.) Yarn over. Pull up a loop. There will be two loops on the hook.

The photo below shows the hook poking out the back.

3. Repeat Step 2 in each stitch across (except for the far left bar), adding a loop to the hook with each stitch.

4. To work the final stitch, identify the final vertical bar and the horizontal thread that runs behind it. Insert the hook so it is behind both of these threads. When viewed from the side, the two threads look like a backwards 6 for right-handers and a regular 6 for lefties.

> **NOTE** Even though you are working in Tunisian knit stitch, the final stitch is a Tunisian simple stitch. This creates stability along the left side.

Yarn over, pull up a loop. Count the loops. You should have the same number as you did on the foundation row.

5. Work standard return.

The photo shows Tunisian knit stitch fabric.

Here is what it looks like on the back.

Tunisian Purl Stitch

Work foundation row forward and return. Look at the finished stitches. You will see a vertical bar for each stitch. These bars are what you will pick up as you work the Tunisian purl stitch forward pass. Keep the hook to the front of the work, as you did in Tunisian simple stitch.

Forward Pass

1. Skip the first vertical bar that is on the far right side, directly below the hook. Bring the yarn to the front of the work.

2. Insert the hook into the next vertical bar, keeping the hook to the front of the work. The photo shows the yarn being held in place by my right index finger.

3. Let the yarn go. Bring it toward you in front of the stitch then back under the hook.

4. Yarn over, pull up a loop with that yarn. There will be two loops on the hook.

5. Repeat Step 1 in each stitch across (except for the far left bar), adding a loop to the hook with each stitch. Notice the "purl bump" in the front of each stitch.

6. To work the final stitch, identify the final vertical bar and the horizontal thread that runs behind it.

> **NOTE** You will work a Tunisian simple stitch into the final stitch, not a Tunisian purl stitch. Do not move the yarn to the front of the hook.

Insert the hook so it is behind both of these threads. When viewed from the side, the two threads look like a backwards *6* for right-handers and a regular *6* for lefties.

Yarn over, pull up a loop. Count the loops. You should have the same number as you did on the foundation row.

7. Work standard return.

The photo shows Tunisian purl fabric.

Change Colors or Start New Yarn

Sometimes you will need to change colors for a stripe pattern. You will also need to start a new ball of yarn when the previous one runs out. The method is the same in both cases.

The ideal place to start a new yarn is at the end of a return pass.

1. Work return pass until two loops remain on hook. Drop first yarn to the back. Yarn over with new yarn.

Pull through both loops.

Pull old and new tails firmly to hold stitches in place.

2. Continue working with the new yarn, making sure you are using the working end of the yarn and not the short tail.

Final Row

The top row of Tunisian crochet looks looser than the previous rows because nothing is worked into it. One way to end the piece neatly is to work single crochet stitches across the top of that row.

1. Insert your hook as you would for whatever stitch pattern you're using. In the example, this is Tunisian simple stitch.

2. Yarn over, pull up loop, yarn over, pull through two loops. This creates a single crochet.

3. Repeat Step 2 across.

Helpful Hints

- Never turn your work. The right side is always facing you.
- Always skip the first vertical bar.
- Pull the yarn snug at the start of each row to keep the edge from getting baggy.
- The final stitch on every forward pass should be a Tunisian simple stitch, regardless of the other stitches on that row.
- Work the final stitch on the forward pass into the vertical bar and the horizontal bar behind it for stability. If you turn that edge toward you, those two threads should look like a backwards 6 for right-handers and a regular 6 for lefties.
- Make sure you count the last stitch of the forward pass and the first stitch of the return pass separately.

- You can work any stitch into any other type of stitch (for example, Tunisian purl stitch into Tunisian knit stitch, or Tunisian simple stitch into Tunisian purl stitch, and so on).
- Count! Check your stitch count regularly to make sure you did not miss picking up a stitch on a forward pass or mistakenly pull through the wrong number of loops on a return pass.
- To reduce the curl in Tunisian crochet, work the foundation row into the back bumps of the starting chains. To eliminate any remaining curl, gently steam block your finished pieces.

Stuffing and
Closing Pillows

Prefabricated pillow forms come in several styles and materials. Some have knife edges while others have a box shape. Forms can be squishy or firm. I recommend washable, nonallergenic, flame-retardant pillows you can find in craft and sewing stores. If they don't have the size you're looking for, you can have dense foam custom cut for a reasonable price. It's a good idea to wait until your crocheted cover is done then take it with you when you shop for a form. That way you can be sure to get the size you need.

It is important that your pillow form be 1 to 2 inches (2.5 to 5.1 centimeters) larger than your crocheted pillow cover. This ensures that the corners will be full and the pillow will be nice and plump.

You can also repurpose an existing pillow as the stuffing for a new one.

With the exception of the small spiral flower, I do not recommend polyester fiberfill because it tends to clump, especially if you run it through the wash.

I use two methods to close the pillows in this book: (1) crochet them all the way around or (2) use multipart construction so the pillow form can be slipped in and out. Either method would work for any of the patterns in the book. If, however, you prefer a different technique, like sewing in a zipper or using hook-and-loop fabric, feel free to use it.

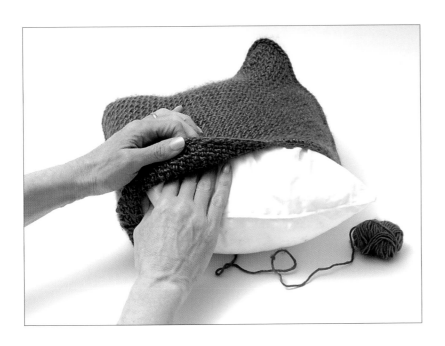

Resources

STANDARDS & GUIDELINES FOR CROCHET AND KNITTING

Standard Yarn Weight System

Categories of yarn, gauge ranges, and recommended needle and hook sizes

Yarn Weight Symbol & Category Names	1 Super Fine	2 Fine	3 Light	4 Medium	5 Bulky	6 Super Bulky
Type of Yarns in Category	Sock, Fingering, Baby	Sport, Baby	DK, Light Worsted	Worsted, Afghan, Aran	Chunky, Craft, Rug	Bulky, Roving
Knit Gauge Range* in Stockinette Stitch to 4 inches	27–32 sts	23–26 sts	21–24 sts	16–20 sts	12–15 sts	6–11 sts
Recommended Needle in Metric Size Range	2.25–3.25 mm	3.25–3.75 mm	3.75–4.5 mm	4.5–5.5 mm	5.5–8 mm	8 mm and larger
Recommended Needle U.S. Size Range	1 to 3	3 to 5	5 to 7	7 to 9	9 to 11	11 and larger
Crochet Gauge* Ranges in Single Crochet to 4 inch	21–32 sts	16–20 sts	12–17 sts	11–14 sts	8–11 sts	5–9 sts
Recommended Hook in Metric Size Range	2.25–3.5 mm	3.5–4.5 mm	4.5–5.5 mm	5.5–6.5 mm	6.5–9 mm	9 mm and larger
Recommended Hook U.S. Size Range	B–1 to E–4	E–4 to 7	7 to I–9	I–9 to K–10½	K–10½ to M–13	M–13 and larger

* GUIDELINES ONLY: The above reflect the most commonly used gauges and needle or hook sizes for specific yarn categories.

SKILL LEVELS FOR CROCHET

1 ◖□□▷ **Beginner**	Projects for first-time crocheters using basic stitches. Minimal shaping.
2 ◖■□▷ **Easy**	Projects using yarn with basic stitches, repetitive stitch patterns, simple color changes, and simple shaping and finishing.
3 ◖■■▷ **Intermediate**	Projects using a variety of techniques, such as basic lace patterns or color patterns, mid-level shaping and finishing.
4 ◖■■▶ **Experienced**	Projects with intricate stitch patterns, techniques and dimension, such as non-repeating patterns, multicolor techniques, fine threads, small hooks, detailed shaping and refined finishing.

This Standards & Guidelines booklet and downloadable symbol artwork are available at: **YarnStandards.com**

Books

Barnden, Betty. *The Crochet Stitch Bible.* Iola, WI: Krause Publications, 2004.

Callahan, Gail. *Hand Dyeing Yarn and Fleece.* North Adams, MA: Storey Publishing, LLC, 2010.

Christmas, Carolyn and Dorris Brooks. *101 Easy Tunisian Stitches.* Berne, IN: Annie's Attic, 2004.

Eckman, Edie. *The Crochet Answer Book.* North Adams, MA: Storey Publishing, 2005.

Grabowski, Angela "ARNie." *Encyclopedia of Tunisian Crochet.* Abilene, TX: LoneStar Abilene Publishing, LLC, 2004.

Matthews, Anne. *Vogue Dictionary of Crochet Stitches.* Newton, UK: David & Charles, 1987.

Reader's Digest. *The Ultimate Sourcebook of Knitting and Crochet Stitches.* Pleasantville, NY: Reader's Digest, 2003.

Silverman, Sharon Hernes. *Basic Crocheting.* Mechanicsburg, PA: Stackpole Books, 2006.

Silverman, Sharon Hernes. *Beyond Basic Crocheting.* Mechanicsburg, PA: Stackpole Books, 2007.

Silverman, Sharon Hernes. *Tunisian Crochet.* Mechanicsburg, PA: Stackpole Books, 2009.

Yarn

Abuelita Yarns
www.abuelitayarns.com

Blue Heron Yarns
www.blueheronyarns.com

Jojoland
www.jojoland.com

Kangaroo Dyer
www.kangaroodyer.com

Lion Brand Yarn Company
www.lionbrand.com

Louet North America
www.louet.com

Plymouth Yarn Company, Inc.
www.plymouthyarn.com

Tahki Stacy Charles, Inc.
www.tahkistacycharles.com

Hooks

ChiaoGoo/Westing Bridge LLC
www.chiaogoo.com

Denise Interchangeable Knitting and Crochet
www.knitdenise.com

Stitch Diva Studios
www.stitchdiva.com

Other Resources

CRAFT YARN COUNCIL OF AMERICA (CYCA)

The craft yarn industry's trade association has educational links and free projects.
www.craftyarncouncil.com

CROCHET GUILD OF AMERICA (CGOA)

The national association for crocheters, CGOA sponsors conventions, offers correspondence courses, and maintains a membership directory.
www.crochet.org

CROCHET INSIDER
www.crochetinsider.com

GETTING LOOPY
http://gettingloopy.com

INTERWEAVE PRESS
www.interweave.com

THE NATIONAL NEEDLEARTS ASSOCIATION (TNNA)

This international trade organization represents retailers, manufacturers, distributors, designers, manufacturers' representatives, publishers, teachers, and wholesalers of products and supplies for the specialty needlearts market.
www.tnna.org

NEXSTITCH
www.nexstitch.com

RAVELRY

This free online community for knitters, crocheters, and other fiber fans is *the* place to exchange information, manage projects, get advice on techniques, and keep up with everything yarn related.
www.ravelry.com

STITCH DIVA STUDIOS
www.stitchdiva.com

TUNISIAN CROCHET GROUP
http://groups.yahoo.com/group/tunisiancrochet/

YARN THING
http://knitting.blogspot.com

Visual Index

Springtime Miters, 2

Sophisticated Chevrons, 5

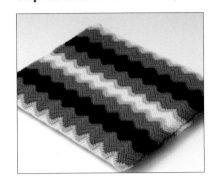

Woven Floor Pillow, 9

Loop-de-loop, 12

Furry Fun, 16

Cable Columns, 19

Sunburst, 24

Spiral Flower, 29

Thanksgiving Bounty, 33

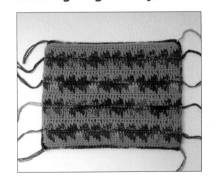

Three-D Squares, 37

Red Hot Heart, 42

Checkerboard, 46

Lovejoy, 50

Beaded Castanets, 57

Royal Purple, 62

Santorini, 67

Debonair, 71

Sweet Dreams, 75

Honeycomb Bolster, 80

Café au Lait, 85